# THE ART OF

# Practicing Law

# THE ART OF

## *Practicing Law*

## TALKING TO CLIENTS, COLLEAGUES AND OTHERS

### JAMES M. KRAMON

**ABA**

Cover design by Kelly Book/ABA Publishing.

Printed in the United States of America

16  15  14  13  12    5 4 3 2 1

**Library of Congress Cataloging-in-Publication Data**

Kramon, James M.
   The art of practicing law / James M. Kramon.
      p. cm.
   Includes index.
   ISBN 978-1-61438-425-0
   1. Practice of law—United States. 2. Lawyers—United States. I. Title.
   KF300.K73   2012
   347.73'0504—dc23

                                                              2012008240

Discounts are available for books ordered in bulk. Special consideration is given to state bars, CLE programs, and other bar-related organizations. Inquire at Book Publishing, ABA Publishing, American Bar Association, 321 North Clark Street, Chicago, Illinois 60654-7598.

www.ShopABA.org

To the memory of Paula

and for Justin and Annie

# Foreword

THE REMINISCENCES OF MY fellow lawyers—I have read more than my share—run to type. Some are gripping and some are tedious. But they typically focus on the external—the trial of public interest, the celebrated client, the historic context. Not infrequently, they underscore the authors' lawyering skills.

Jim Kramon has broken that mold and has added a fresh and welcome dimension to the genre. *The Art of Practicing Law* is not a highlights reel. It is intensely personal and essentially modest—an intimate and highly readable account of dozens of "backstories" drawn from otherwise unremarkable encounters in Kramon's daily practice of law.

The short vignettes in *The Art of Practicing Law* look inward—to the impact that encounters with clients, interested parties and mere bystanders have on the author. They record lessons learned about law and life and reflect insights into the endless play of the human comedy. They show us interactions with charlatans, saints and deadbeats, and present the ethical conundrums of an advocate wrestling with "truth." Of particular interest to lawyers who, like Kramon, came to the Bar in a pre-computer age, they include some nostalgic meditations, including one on the quiet majesty of law libraries, places where those who choose to listen can hear the silent rhythms of the law.

In his introduction, Kramon asserts that he tried but failed to define a "connective tissue" that links the many incidents he describes. All that connects them, he says, "is the emotional impact of the incidents on me." To this reader, however, Kramon's book contains an overarching theme: we advance the rule of law even in the routine practice of our profession, and, in so doing, we acquire wisdom, often from the most unlikely sources. It is not too much to say that Kramon's book illustrates that even in the quotidian practice we may, in Holmes' phrase, "live greatly in the law."

Kramon's reflections are unsparingly honest and written in a lively and vigorous style. They are frequently marked by passages of beauty. They are certain to inform, instruct and entertain lawyer and layman alike.

*The Art of Practicing Law* is a valuable, and novel, contribution to the literature of lawyer reminiscence.

Stephen H. Sachs
Attorney General of Maryland, 1979–1987
United States Attorney for the District of Maryland, 1967–1970

ò&

# Contents

## ❧ CHAPTER TWO
### Others    77

## ❧ CHAPTER THREE

## ❧ CHAPTER FOUR

# Introduction

JOKES ABOUT LAWYERS DESCRIBE them as dull and tedious. The jokes suggest that lawyers are dispassionate, that they don't show emotions the way other people do. So far as the public persona of members of my profession is concerned, the jokes have it about right. Spectacular cases aside, lawyers don't get high grades for dramatic effect.

But the point is more complicated than the jokes suggest. Practicing law presents many dramatic situations. The difficulty is that these situations don't often present themselves in the public aspects of practicing law. They are the "backstories" that occur in unseen parts of our work. It is in private meetings with clients and others, in behind-the-scenes events and personal reflections that the emotional experiences of my profession are found. This book is about such experiences.

Every situation I describe in the essays that follow occurred in my practice of law. Frequently a backstory engaged me more than the case within which it arose and, over time, proved to be more memorable. Feelings of clients revealed in the privacy of my office were often more moving than the legal matters that brought the clients to me. Events involving others with whom I interacted in the course of my work sometimes were fascinating even when the work involved was otherwise not particularly interesting. My meeting with Governor George Wallace, perhaps the most notorious racist of the twentieth century, in his hospital room after he was shot and paralyzed is far more memorable than the case against the strange young man who shot him. I tell about such incidents in this book.

For a long time I tried to define the connective tissue that unites the cases and contemplative moments in which a backstory arose. Those attempts failed. I came to realize that what connects these situations is not the cases but the emotional effect of each situation on me. The stories described here occurred in cases that received national attention and cases that attracted no attention whatsoever. They covered a wide range of areas of law and were large and small, complex and simple, criminal and civil. The backstories transcend the specific cases in which they occurred.

I discuss music, painting, architecture, ethics, and other subjects encountered in my work. I describe clients who found themselves in unusual situations and clients whose personalities were, to say the least, idiosyncratic. I offer the private thoughts of a lawyer, some generous and some critical, as he performs his work. It would be dishonest not to say that this book is as much a selective memoir as it is a collection of essays about incidents I encountered in my practice. I have chosen stories that interested me and captured my emotional response. The legal issues in the cases I selected are less important than the feelings of the people involved, myself included.

Two provisos: First, I have changed names, personal descriptions and immaterial details when necessary to preserve professional confidences. Second, I have rearranged incidents and specific facts when doing so better expressed the point of a particular essay.

# CHAPTER ONE

# Clients

# Preface

CLIENTS ARE THE MOST important, difficult and interesting aspect of practicing law. Unlike others with whom lawyers deal, clients and lawyers expose and frequently exaggerate their good and bad qualities when dealing with one another. The lawyer-client relationship requires clients to address issues of dependence, trust, fear and truthfulness. It requires lawyers to address issues of competence, responsibility and professionalism. To ignore such issues would reduce lawyers to functionaries and their work to formulaic selection of responses to legal problems.

Clients are not important simply because they engage and pay lawyers. They are important because even the most exquisite understanding of legal principles has no meaning without applying those principles to the situations of clients. Law is, after all, an applied science. Its vitality grows out of its ability to apply legal principles to facts and circumstances confronting a particular individual. Thus, the personality and idiosyncrasies of each client affect a lawyer's choice of appropriate legal principles and strategies. A lawyer does not give the same advice about testifying to a shy, reticent client and a poised, convincing one. A lawyer does not treat possibilities for resolving a dispute in the same manner for a wealthy, idle client and a busily engaged client on a limited budget.

The intimacy of the attorney-client relationship distinguishes it from others. Clients are generally forthcoming and reveal confidences to lawyers for several reasons. One reason is that candor with a lawyer is important to get the best possible legal services. Another is that clients are aware of the privileged nature of the lawyer-client relationship. There is also a third reason that I have never been able to explain accurately. It has something to do with a client's implicit admission that by coming to a lawyer he or she is in need of assistance or advice from someone else.

The essays that follow describe clients I have served in my legal practice. Each client I discuss was in a unique situation but their characteristics and feelings would differ even if their situations were identical. People may have similar qualities, but I have never had two clients who expressed themselves in identical ways to their lawyer. The range of personalities a lawyer encounters with clients is infinite.

I have selected for this book incidents involving clients that seem to me to transcend the particular case involved. The common denominator of the incidents I have selected is that I found them emotional and memorable. It is interesting to me that such incidents occurred as often in cases involving unremarkable clients as they did in cases involving famous or unusual clients. My experience has been that no particular group of people has a monopoly on special events and feelings.

ᘓ ᘓ ᘓ

# Racial Discrimination

I LIKED HAROLD ROBERTS the first time he came to my office and I liked him more as we got to know each other. Harold had a very pleasant self-contained personality and I liked him especially because he gave me the opportunity to play out every lawyer's secret dream of pretending to be Atticus Finch. Although Harold wasn't accused of committing a crime, his case involved unvarnished discrimination against a black man.

Harold's story was simple and he told it to me without rancor or bitterness.

Harold's file as an employee of a county Department of Transportation was virtually perfect. Every one of Harold's reviews contained nothing other than favorable comments. There wasn't a single blemish on his record. Harold had, however, hit a glass ceiling.

On three occasions Harold had applied for a posted job at a higher level and been denied it. On each occasion, his score on the qualifying exam was the highest of all applicants. On each occasion, the job was given to a white man with clearly inferior credentials. Were I Harold, I would have conferred with a lawyer after the first denial. I asked him why he waited until the third denial before doing so. Harold told me that until it occurred three times he thought it was possible there were other reasons why someone else got the promotion. Harold wasn't a man who assumed prejudice easily.

Believing completely in a client's case, feeling outrage at those who have violated him, is a rare privilege for a lawyer. I have seldom been outraged by the conduct of my adversaries. Disrespect or a belief that someone acted incorrectly is far from outrage. That a man as fine as Harold was discriminated against by a county agency is an outrage.

There were no overt acts or writings to support the claim of racial prejudice. No one had used offensive epithets in addressing Harold or speaking about him to others insofar as we knew. There were no "smoking gun" documents clearly suggesting intentional racial discrimination in the Department of Transportation.

The Department's statistics, however, which were kept in compliance with federal law for a number of years, clearly indicated that black employees were not promoted above a certain grade level. Since the Department had many black employees, and there were no arguable reasons for this, it was obvious from these statistics we would prevail if there were to be a trial.

There was, as it turned out, no trial. The county agreed to an acceptable settlement, giving Harold his choice of moving to the higher grade with retroactive compensation adjustment or simply receiving a cash settlement and leaving the Department of Transportation's employ. Exhausted and fed up by the entire process, Harold chose the latter. Shortly thereafter, I helped Harold establish a small business that served him well.

❧ ❧ ❧

# Bequest with Deceased Husband

AN ELDERLY WIDOW ARRIVES at my office too formally dressed to do a simple codicil to her will. I told her when she telephoned we could do our work together by phone, but she insisted on coming to see me personally. I offer her coffee or tea, which she declines, and notice as she takes her seat that she appears to be only partly engaged. There is a wistful quality about her as she tells me she has decided to leave a particular painting to her son-in-law. My client and her late husband apparently had reservations about him, which over the years dissipated. She speaks affectionately of her son-in-law as she tells me how much he admired the painting she will be leaving him.

As my client explains what she wishes to do, in far more detail than required to do the codicil, I become aware she is not speaking as though she were alone. Her repeated use of "we" and "our" and her frequent glances at an imaginary person in the empty chair beside her signify clearly that in her mind her late husband is with her. They have come to satisfactory terms with their son-in-law and they are making a gift of the painting together.

 governance governance governance

# A Tugboat Operator

I FIRST MET MY client, Chester Rathskeller, at the office of his employer's lawyer. Chester, a tugboat operator, worked for a towing company. He was a slight man dressed in overalls with an expressionless, pasty white face. Chester was charged by the Coast Guard with negligently obstructing a navigable channel, causing a collision with an ocean freighter. He had fallen asleep returning from nearly two days of uninterrupted towing operations. The accident resulted in serious injuries to four people and significant damage to the freighter.

Two questions came to mind when I first saw Chester: How could so unimposing a man be responsible for such extensive damage? How could he be permitted to perform towing procedures unassisted? I pondered these questions as Chester and I walked from his employer's lawyer's office to my own, a block and a half away.

The facts of the case were simple: Chester was returning to the company's boatyard after he completed his extensive assignments. The return route was easy to follow, but it required tugboats to cross the deep navigable channel. While the tugboat was proceeding on this route, Chester left the controls for a moment to go below and get a cup of coffee.

Chester needed that cup of coffee on the night in question, having gone nearly 48 hours with no sleep because of the large number of ships that required towing. His offense, if you can call it that, was to fall asleep while trying to get a cup of coffee. When he awoke at the sound of the collision, he was horrified to see the damage it had caused. Coast Guard officials who arrived a short time later stated that Chester was in an obvious state of shock, trying to gather scattered parts by leaning over the back of the tugboat. Chester had no recollection of doing that.

Chester was virtually emotionless as he told me the story. When he finished, I told him I wanted to visit the tugboat and we did so later that day. The deck and rigging of the tug were pretty much what I had expected, but the room below deck was worse than I ever imagined. The airless fetid room made the rooms Solzhenitsyn described in the Gulag look like at least a three-star hotel. In this foul-smelling place were the remains of a folding card table, an easy chair of the sort you see abandoned on the side of the road, a coffee pot that undoubtedly survived at least one world war, a seatless toilet that I will not describe further, and a small pile of girlie magazines. Chester's mug and spilled coffee were on the floor near the coffee pot. After two minutes of holding my breath in the room I told Chester that I had seen enough and we should go back on deck.

There was little to rehearse with Chester for the Coast Guard hearing. Everyone agreed that the accident resulted from his falling asleep. I wanted the Administrative Law Judge conducting the hearing to know that Chester had worked nearly all of the previous two days, that he was operating the tug unassisted, and that the conditions his job required him to endure were abysmal. Because such hearings are relatively informal the Coast Guard's lawyer did not object to questions about these matters.

When Chester appeared at the hearing it was as if a sanitation worker had inadvertently been invited to the Queen's ball. He was the only person in the hearing room not wearing a suit and tie. Other than when he testified—with the flattest affect imaginable—Chester did not speak during the hearing. He asked no questions and made no comments in response to anything said. The Administrative Law Judge gave his verdict immediately after closing arguments. Chester's work document, a necessity for his job as a tugboat operator, was cancelled and he would be ineligible to reapply for at least one year.

The accident received a great deal of publicity. Anyone following it would picture Chester as a negligent tugboat operator who had no concern for the damage and injury he had caused. Anyone learning of the verdict would infer from the publicity that Chester got off easy.

The publicity said nothing about the Chester Rathskeller I represented. It did not tell the public how guileless a man he was. It did not tell the public how hard he worked and how difficult a task he was called upon to perform alone. It did not tell anything about the barren dungeon that provided him with the only place to get a cup of coffee.

To make the situation worse, I learned during the case that safety devices with audible warnings that could have prevented the accident were available at nominal cost. The Coast Guard did not require the use of such devices.

≈ ≈ ≈

# A Boring Client

I'M MEETING THIS MORNING with my client, Hugh Finley. Hugh owns a small men's store of the sort rapidly vanishing. Hugh is married and he and his wife have three children. I assume that his interaction with others is very limited. He comes to me every few months to review various business matters. The matters consist largely of complaints by customers who have purchased clothes at Hugh's store. We have reviewed each type of complaint many times and I have offered to supply Hugh with form letters that would eliminate the need for coming to me. Nevertheless, Hugh insists upon reviewing every complaint with me.

The meetings Hugh insists upon would be tedious enough without an additional factor. The additional factor is that Hugh is probably the most boring person I have ever met. If the average personality ranges from 0 to 100, Hugh's personality ranges from 48 to 52. He has no highs or lows and his brief divergences from our work generally concern subjects so mundane as to make it difficult to respond.

As Hugh's lawyer I accept him as he is, but can't help feeling sorry for him because of his lack of personality. Although I find it difficult to stay awake in my meetings with Hugh, I do my best to make him feel I'm interested in what we are discussing. I wouldn't want to go to a doctor who let me know that she was bored to tears with the sort of medical problem for which I came to her.

In addition to trying my best to look interested and taking a few notes that actually serve no purpose, I've found a particular approach that works well to assure Hugh that I'm interested in what he is saying. The approach I use is quite simple. In listening to Hugh's litany I select a remark that lends itself to a reasonable question. After waiting several minutes, I say to Hugh "let me take you back to where you said. . . ." Then I ask the question I have decided upon.

This approach does several things for Hugh. First, it lets him know I'm listening to what he is saying. Second, it lets him know I'm thinking about a solution to the problem and want to be certain I have the facts straight. One could say this approach is somewhat disingenuous, but with a client such as Hugh I believe it's appropriate. One of my responsibilities to Hugh is to convince him that what he has to say is worthwhile and I'm treating it as worthy of consideration:

"Hugh, did I understand you to say a few minutes ago that you knew Mrs. Cummings was going to complain about the items she purchased?"

Hugh responds to my question by saying, "I've learned there's a type of person who is always dissatisfied with her purchase. I'd like to tell people like that not to buy anything, but I can't do that."

I respond, "I guess after many years in business you develop a sixth sense for customers who will cause problems. It must be awful to sell something to someone you know will be complaining about it."

Hugh is satisfied with our little colloquy. When he leaves my office he feels there's someone who finds what he has to say interesting enough to listen to it and ask a question. I've done something for Hugh in addition to providing him with a good response to Mrs. Cummings' complaint.

۶ۈ  ۶ۈ  ۶ۈ

## Selling the Family Farm

A CLIENT OF MINE, Samuel Morrison, is a rather stiff businessman who lives in a suburb of Washington with his wife and two children. Sam was once described to me by a business associate as being "so tight he squeaks." I meet with Sam every month or two to review miscellaneous legal matters pertaining to his business. Sam is a pleasant but somewhat withheld man and I have never felt I have gotten to know him.

On this occasion, Sam has come to my office for another purpose. His father, having survived his wife, has just succumbed to a lengthy illness. Sam is the executor of his father's estate and he has brought his father's will, prepared by a Virginia lawyer years ago, to our meeting. The will provides for the division of the estate among the three children in equal shares. Sam has a younger sister living in New York and married to a doctor and an older unmarried brother living in North Carolina. The three siblings are on good terms, although they do not see one another often.

I have asked a young lawyer who recently joined our firm to join us at our meeting. I have never been favorably impressed by him, but have not worked with him sufficiently to be able to say why I feel this way. Before the meeting I explain the background and the sorts of interactions I've had with Sam over the years. I explain that the purpose of our meeting is to explore the estate of Sam's father and determine what Sam is required to do in his capacity as executor.

When we take our seats in the conference room, Sam is on the opposite side of a long conference table that runs between us. He is facing the exterior glass wall of the building, which the young lawyer and I have at our backs. The daylight entering the room illuminates the features of Sam's face.

After a brief exchange of pleasantries, we get down to business. The will is easy to understand and what we must accomplish in order to effectuate it properly is clear. The problem, however, is the diversity of assets in the estate—cash, stocks, bonds, the proceeds of an insurance policy, a few ongoing payments, and the family farm in rural Virginia.

The first part of our discussion concerns the mechanics of the probate process. It doesn't take long to cover this matter and we proceed to discuss the division of the assets in the estate. It is clear that in order for each of the three siblings to receive shares of equal value, the farm will need to be divided or sold. Sam's rough estimate of the values of the estate's assets suggests the farm comprises about half of the estate's total value. Since maintaining a farm the size of the Morrison farm, perhaps seventy-five acres, is difficult to justify economically and since Sam's siblings have no interest in any portion of it, there is an assumption that the farm will be sold.

Less than an hour into our meeting, it becomes obvious to me that the young lawyer isn't paying attention to our client. I can see his notes, which are sketchy and ill-considered. I also see him periodically look away from the conversation I'm having with Sam. The young lawyer's lack of interest is getting on my nerves.

The first time I mention selling the farm I notice that the tip of Sam's nose turns red and the light coming into the conference room glistens on his eyes. I'm reasonably certain that Sam is struggling to maintain composure.

We leave the subject of the farm for several minutes and return to it with a question clearly suggesting once again that the farm will be sold. This time Sam is overwhelmed and pretends that something is making him sneeze. He pulls his handkerchief out of his pocket and wipes his nose and eyes. To relieve his embarrassment, I go to the door of the conference room and ask my secretary to bring us more coffee.

Before we finish our meeting there's a third occasion when Sam becomes emotional at the mention of selling the farm. It is obvious what is occurring each time the subject is raised and I decide to discuss it with the young lawyer after Sam departs.

I saw the Morrison farm once by happenstance. It is truly a field of dreams. Snuggled in a gracious curve of a rural road passing through gorgeous Virginia horse country, the farm contains a small outbuilding, a barn, two ponds, a number of lush fields of crops, and, of course, the farmhouse. From many of its windows, the view is the foothills of the Blue Mountains in the distance. Fish were jumping in the nearer of the two ponds during my short visit. In the evening when the farm's lights are turned on, as they were on the occasion I saw it, the Morrison farm has a quality about it that makes the world feel right. I could easily fall in love with the Morrison farm, and it is clear to me that someone at our table already has.

We end the meeting shortly and shake hands goodbye. The young lawyer and I remain in the conference room with papers and coffee cups scattered around the table. I tell the young lawyer that we will discuss the meeting immediately, while it is still fresh in our minds. I try to be a good psychiatrist and ask my first question in an open-ended manner: "So, what did you think about Sam?" The young lawyer tells me he thought Sam was a very pleasant man, certainly able do everything necessary in his role as executor of his father's estate, and probably a good business-man. At no point does he mention Sam's emotional response to the subject of selling the farm.

Before I can ask my next question, the young lawyer is off and running with law school lessons. He talks about how subordination will affect the priority of liens on the farm, the warranties the executor would or would not be able to give the farm's purchaser and the possibilities for mitigating the estate tax. I'm getting angry and my next question reveals it: "I'm not asking you to prove that you know something about taxes and secured transactions. I'm asking you about our client, Sam, who sat across the table from us for several hours and is paying hundreds of dollars an hour for our services. I want to know what you noticed about him."

To make a long story short, the young lawyer noticed absolutely nothing about Sam. He didn't see Sam's emotional response to selling the farm. Everything he mentioned about Sam could have been determined without meeting him. I consider for a moment saying something like, "How the hell could you have attended the meeting and not recognized that the idea of selling the farm was emotionally overwhelming for Sam? What were you thinking about while he was speaking?" I didn't say this, I said nothing. I asked him to prepare a memorandum of the meeting and put the file scattered around the conference table back together. Then I left to return to my office, convinced that the young lawyer who accompanied me to the meeting had better find another line of work.

&. &. &.

---

# A Painful Interrogation

MY CLIENT, AN ELDERLY widow, is being questioned relentlessly about documents she signed while her late husband was alive. Her interrogator, Carter Harrison, is the lawyer for her late husband's partner, Peter Swanson. A dispute has arisen, over money of course, between the partner and the estate that has been left to my client.

"Mrs. Talmadge, I show you plaintiff's exhibit number 17, a partnership agreement between Mr. Swanson and your late husband. Do you recognize this document?"

"No."

"Would you please look at the last page of this document and tell me what is contained on it?"

"It contains my late husband's signature and my signature."

"You signed this document, correct?"

"Yes."

"What was the purpose of this document, Mrs. Talmadge?"

"I don't know. My husband told me to sign it."

"Did you know, Mrs. Talmadge, that by signing this document you were obligating yourself to something?"

"I'm not a lawyer. I'm just a wife and I was doing what my husband told me to do."

My adversary has repeated this litany five or six times and, judging by the stack of documents he is using, he intends to do it many times more. I have objected on various grounds, particularly that my adversary is harassing my client, but the judge has allowed every question regarding my client's signature on documents. By the time Mr. Harrison has questioned my client about ten or twelve documents of which she has no knowledge, she begins to cry.

I request a recess and the judge, with obvious reluctance, grants us ten minutes. In the relative privacy of the hallway, my client reveals the depth of her humiliation: "Of course, I didn't know what I was signing, wives never do. Was I to tell my husband I wouldn't sign the documents unless he fully explained them to me? Even if he did, I'm sure I wouldn't have understood them." To get these words out exhausted Mrs. Talmadge's supply of Kleenex. She searched her pocketbook in vain for another package.

The case was settled before the end of trial, as we knew it would be. Once each lawyer had inflicted as much damage as possible on the other side, both lawyers knew how the case was likely to come out. The judge thanked the jurors for their service and dismissed them and instructed the lawyers to prepare settlement documents for the court's approval.

The good news is that there was enough money in the pot to satisfy both parties. The damage Mr. Harrison inflicted upon Mrs. Talmadge by revealing her ignorance of the documents she had signed didn't make much difference in the ultimate settlement. I argued in our settlement discussions that certain crucial documents would be found invalid by the court because of Mrs. Talmadge's ignorance of what she was signing. Mr. Harrison and I knew I would not prevail in this argument if the trial continued.

The Talmadges and the Swansons were once good friends. They had dinners together, occasionally traveled together, and were in many business undertakings together. After the lawsuit, Mrs. Talmadge never again spoke with either of the Swansons. A significant part of her and her late husband's lives was wiped away by the adversity of the lawsuit.

I saw Mrs. Talmadge only once after the case was settled. I couldn't tell whether she regretted the outcome of the lawsuit.

## An Unlikely Fortune

A FRIEND CALLED TO ask if I would give some advice to the man who cleaned his office at night. My friend knew I would be available for that purpose. Although I would not be paid, he assured me that I would learn something very interesting at the meeting.

After spending a few minutes getting to know each other, my friend's nighttime cleaner explained the reason for his visit. He worked as janitor at a large bank during the day and as an office cleaner a few nights a week. During the day he cleaned the offices of senior executives of the bank. On such occasions he would ask casual questions about investing money. He might say, for example, "I've got an extra hundred dollars, Mr. Slocum, and wondered what you think might be a good investment." The executives generally recommended long-term investments in the stock of major corporations. The janitor did this for more than twenty years, during which he saved slightly in excess of $500,000.

When a few people learned what he had done, they not only were amazed but several also advised him to write about his experience. One person gave him a proposed agreement whereby he would provide the information necessary to write a small book and the person providing the agreement would actually write it. He came to me because he wanted a lawyer's advice about the proposed agreement.

The janitor prepared, with assistance, a small brochure explaining how he had accomplished the amazing feat of amassing $500,000. The pamphlet was circulated to customers of the bank and others. Shortly thereafter, with great trepidation, the janitor spoke at a public library in Baltimore and explained how he had acquired his improbable savings. The talk at the library was well attended and he later told me he was amazed that people were listening to him. I was not amazed in the slightest.

⅔ ⅔ ⅔

# Impact of Malpractice Case

I SERVED AS WHAT is known as an "excess attorney" in a malpractice case against an abdominal surgeon. The job of an excess attorney is to do everything possible to keep the damages to be paid by his client within the limit of the client's malpractice insurance policy. If the damages exceed that limit, the client is forced to pay the difference out of the client's pocket.

The case against my client was straightforward and, unfortunately, his negligence was clear. The patient, a woman, had an anatomical anomaly that made the surgery to correct an inguinal hernia particularly difficult. While performing the operation, my client lost what is known as the "anatomical plane," which is the reference by which a surgeon knows where to cut. The loss of the anatomical plane resulted in my client's nicking a nearby major nerve. Although the nerve was not severed, enough damage was done to result in significant symptoms. There had been no discussion between my client and his patient after she suffered the injury, which would cause her pain and swelling for the rest of her life. Her lawsuit sought damages in excess of $5,000,000.00. My client's insurance policy had a limit of $1,000,000.00.

The only way I could be certain that this case could be resolved within the coverage of the malpractice insurance policy was for a settlement to be negotiated. At trial, anything could happen, but I doubted that a settlement could be negotiated in light of my client's clear negligence and the severity of the symptoms the patient would endure.

My client appeared to understand the situation, but he could not live with words in the complaint such as "failed to exercise a reasonable degree of care" and "violated his duty to provide his patient with medical services satisfying the standard of care expected of an abdominal surgeon." These words were repeated over and over in the complaint and in various legal documents that followed it. My client told me countless times that he was never negligent, that he had never failed to live up to the expected standard of care. Although his hope was totally unrealistic, my client wanted to be vindicated in a court proceeding.

The job of obtaining a satisfactory settlement in such a case required making contradictory arguments to the lawyer for the injured woman and my client's malpractice insurance company. To the injured woman's lawyer I argued that there were flaws in his client's case and it could easily be lost at trial. In a chameleonlike reversal, I argued to the insurance company that there was no possible way the injured woman could fail to recover more than $1,000,000.00 in a trial. My job was to convince the company that its failure to offer the full amount of the insurance coverage would jeopardize my client with an excess verdict and thereby make the insurance company responsible for declining to settle for $1,000,000.00.

Lawyers are no strangers to making contradictory arguments and there is no duplicity involved in such advocacy. I made each argument as strongly as possible and both the injured woman's lawyer and the insurance company were persuaded to grant my requests. As a result, my client's case was settled for $1,000,000.00 and he had no personal liability.

This would have been a good result except for a phone call I received the following Monday. My client told me with obvious urgency that he had to see me before the end of the day. We made an appointment for late afternoon and he showed up at my office early. He was more sloppily dressed than I had ever seen him and his face was ashen. With no introduction, he cut to the chase: "I've decided to stop practicing surgery. The accusations made against me by my patient and her lawyer couldn't have hurt me more. I will not risk going through that again. I practice medicine as carefully as I can, and once in a while things happen even to the best surgeons. No one should have to suffer as I did going through this case."

I tried to dissuade him, even though I knew my efforts would be fruitless. This was the second time in my experience that a physician client gave up clinical practice after a lawsuit that was resolved satisfactorily.

⅔ ⅔ ⅔

# An Offensive Client

A CLIENT I WORK for occasionally, Simon Greenwald, has two distinctions: He is the fattest and the nastiest client I have ever had.

Ordinarily a person's appearance has nothing to do with our relationship. Obesity is hardly a scarce commodity among people who deal with me. I had an obesity-related experience with this client, however, that was downright scary.

We were on our way back to our offices after a visit to a bank about an hour away. As we drove past a Chinese restaurant with which Simon was familiar, he suggested we stop for lunch. Since it was nearly two o'clock in the afternoon and I had not eaten anything substantial that day, I welcomed his suggestion. We parked and went into the restaurant. After several minutes spent looking at the menu, we ordered appetizers and main dishes. What arrived was, by my standards, a fairly large amount of food. We finished it off in approximately a half hour during which we also discussed what we had seen at the bank.

The frightening part of this experience began when the check arrived. Simon turned to me and said, "Would you mind if I ordered one more thing?" The question seemed strange since we had just finished a full meal, but I didn't want to offend Simon and so said, "No, order what you like." I declined his offer to order something else for myself. His dish arrived about 10 minutes later, served on an ornate platter. Almost instantly, Simon picked up the serving platter and poured its entire contents onto the clean plate the waiter had provided. He immediately began eating his extra meal with a fervor I have seen only in famished dogs. As he ate, or, more accurately, shoveled the food into his mouth, I noticed beads of sweat appearing on his forehead. I doubt it took more than three minutes for Simon to consume the entire dish.

A minute or two later Simon asked again, "Do you mind if I order something else?" This time I was amazed. I was even more amazed when it happened yet a third time.

After consuming three additional dinner dishes, Simon was drenched in perspiration and appeared to be hyperventilating. Fearing he was about to collapse, I suggested we leave the restaurant and get in the car. We paid our check, and left. Simon struggled to make it to my car parked a half block away. On our way back to our offices, he fell asleep and snored loudly. I wasn't certain whether to drive to our offices or to a hospital. I knew Simon visited a weight-reduction hospital for several weeks every year; he referred to it as a "fat farm." I wondered whether this might be a good time for a visit.

The nasty experience I had with Simon also occurred at a restaurant. I was introducing Simon to two clients who needed the particular financial services Simon provided. One client was an orthodontist, the other a builder of small suburban office buildings. We met in front of the restaurant and I made the introductions.

From the minute the conversation began I saw that Simon was angry. He began making remarks to my clients that were so rude I couldn't believe what I was hearing. "Larry, you don't know enough to ask that question. In fact, you don't know enough to come in out of the rain." "Herb, if you want to do this sort of project, you'd better sharpen your pencil. If you think the kind of crap that gets you through your buildings will work in this area, forget it."

While Simon was looking away, Herb gave Larry a wink and then said, "Simon, I really appreciate your frankness. One of the reasons Larry and I wanted to meet you is that you have a no-bullshit reputation. We need the kind of criticism you're giving us and really appreciate the time you're taking."

Larry took his cue. "Simon, I couldn't agree with Herb more. We're going to invest a lot of hard-earned money in this project and we don't want to flush it down the drain. We don't need any stroking. We need the candor you're giving us." Larry's remarks to Simon were followed by another round of false expressions of gratitude and Simon never caught on.

Simon left the restaurant to attend a meeting "with people who, at least, know what they're doing." A few minutes later Larry, Herb and I left, and I tried to apologize for Simon's behavior. Larry's comment pretty well summed things up: "Forget it. We were the ones who asked to meet him. Is he always a total asshole?"

≈ ≈ ≈

# A Sheriff's Testimony

MY CLIENT, A SHERIFF who lived and worked in the mountains of western Maryland, stood trial for allegedly being an unregistered "dealer" in firearms. The charge was false.

My client was what is called a "country boy." He had lived in the same rural area all his life and his friends had been his friends forever. His wife, who accompanied him to my office and to court, almost never spoke. On those rare occasions when she did, she was as self-effacing as a chambermaid in Buckingham Palace.

The case for the prosecution lasted two and a half days. Two agents of the Bureau of Alcohol, Tobacco, and Firearms testified that they had seen my client buy and sell guns to different people. I knew with certainty that my client had never been a "dealer" of any sort, and his purchases and sales of guns had been casual transactions between friends. Within his small group of friends, exchanging guns for modest sums of money was almost an everyday occurrence.

The case depended upon my client's testimony. I had decided to call him as the first defense witness. He was not prepared to testify even as the prosecutor was finishing his case.

With a lawyer in my firm playing the role of prosecutor, we had rehearsed my client's testimony ten or more times. I had twice taken my client to the federal courtroom where the case would be heard to familiarize him with sitting in the witness box and looking at the jury. It was difficult for me to believe that a man who worked as a Sheriff, and presumably from time to time was called to testify, was so nervous about testifying in his own case. He shook when he botched the words he was trying to say. Once, several weeks before the trial, I asked him if he would speak with his doctor to see whether a tranquilizer might be useful.

When the court adjourned for the evening following the prosecution's next to last witness, I took my client back to my office to try, once again, to get him ready to testify. His wife followed us for the one-block walk from the courthouse to my office building. She sat down in the waiting room as we began to walk down the hall to my office.

This was one of the hardest times I ever experienced as a lawyer. I was certain my client was innocent of the charge he was facing, but I was equally certain that without his respectable testimony he would be convicted. If convicted, he would definitely lose his job as a Sheriff and probably serve at least a short prison sentence. If I or anyone of reasonable ability could have testified for him, he would almost certainly leave the courthouse a free man. Knowing that someone's ability, or inability, to testify—not the facts of the case or the law—would determine whether a life was destroyed was almost too burdensome to bear.

The lawyer who was playing the role of prosecutor came into my office and we began the final rehearsal. As usual, my client was absolutely terrible. For a while, I took the witness stand and played his role as I wanted him to do when questioned by the prosecutor. I asked my client simply to copy how I had testified but he was unable to do so.

Out of frustration, I yelled at my client when he screwed up his lines even after hearing me deliver them minutes before: "You're going to go to jail with that testimony, and there's nothing I can do about it. You're pretty much OK when *I* question you, but when the prosecutor asks you questions, you can't get anything out. For the fiftieth time, the prosecutor is no different from anybody else! All he can do is ask questions and you can answer them just as though they were asked by me. Don't pay attention to anything but the question and answer it the way we have rehearsed it."

I didn't realize how angry I sounded and was taken aback by my client's response: "I can't do what you want. I'm sorry. I just can't." My client then walked out of my office and joined his wife in the waiting room. Since it was evening and not possible to reenter our offices after the outer door closed, my client's future depended on whether we would hear a click from the latch on the door. If we did, then my client and his wife would have left and all would be over. If we didn't, he would return to my office and try again.

Interminable minutes passed and there was no click. Flushed and exhausted, my client reentered my office and immediately took the seat designated for him as witness. "Do it again," he said as he sat down and looked at the lawyer who was playing the role of prosecutor. This time, with his fists so tightly closed I could see the tendons straining in his hands, my client gave passable testimony to the prosecutor. He wouldn't win an award for the performance, but it would be good enough to give me what I needed to make the closing argument I had been rehearsing in my mind for weeks.

The prosecutor finished his case at about noon the next day and the judge adjourned court for lunch. As soon as the afternoon session began,

I called my client to the stand. His performance was identical to the performance he had given the prior evening. It was good enough. After several hours' deliberation the jury acquitted him. His hard work, I told him, was what won him what he deserved. I didn't realize it then, but the Sheriff's case would be one of my favorites for many years.*

---

*After a bench conference with the lawyers, the judge, whom I knew quite well, told me the defense I was trying to establish wouldn't work. As I passed the judge's clerk, however, on my way back to the table, he whispered to me that the jury was going for the defense. Fortunately, the predictions of clerks are nearly always correct.

ॐ ॐ ॐ

# A Sad Client

CYNTHIA BOLTON WAS A very sad woman. She became my client at a friend's insistence that she see a lawyer. Cynthia was middle-aged, single, with almost no living relatives, and the survivor of a kidney transplant. The legal matter she came to me about concerned a dispute with her employer. Not only was Cynthia's job at stake, but the only remnant of her self-respect was also at stake. When she came to me, she needed a warm embrace a lot more than a course in employment law.

It was one of those times when I wished I could deal with clients without feeling their pain. I couldn't do this with the exhausted woman sitting on the other side of my desk, her eyes red-rimmed, her cardigan sweater noticeably clashing with her skirt. Cynthia had clearly given up on trying to look her best, and listening to her I understood her relinquishment of vanity.

We talked about the employment matter for perhaps an hour and a half. She left her employment contract and the relevant letters she had exchanged with her employer with me. I knew I would spend an hour or two that evening reviewing them. After Cynthia left I realized that I had forgotten to discuss my legal fees. I decided to include this information in my letter confirming my engagement by Cynthia. I was preoccupied by thinking about how to solve her employment problem quickly and inexpensively.

From the information Cynthia gave me it was clear that she had one ally of stature in the network of her employer. Although I doubted he would recall it, I had met this man several years before. I recalled his kindness and the good impression he had made, and even before reviewing the documents further, I decided to call him and arrange an appointment. By the end of the afternoon, after a string of phone calls back and forth with his secretary, I had an appointment in five days.

I decided not to tell Cynthia about the appointment until it had taken place. My decision was not based on Cynthia's possible response, but on my desire to be able to tell Cynthia's ally that we were speaking confidentially. Rather than emphasizing the legal implications of a decision by her employer to fire Cynthia, I had decided within a few hours to pursue Cynthia's case by using her ally to garner sympathy for her.

I met with Cynthia's ally at the time scheduled and found that he was more than willing to be of assistance. He suggested, in fact, that he would speak with the people who had final authority on Cynthia's employment. I made three or four suggestions about how he might present her case, but I left his office knowing that her fate would turn on his personal influence with the final authorities. I would not be attending the crucial meeting.

I was certain I had made the right decision in going to Cynthia's ally without first getting into legal issues with her employer. After returning to my office, I telephoned Cynthia and told her about my meeting with her ally. She was concerned but hopeful. Less than a week later, I received a phone call from the ally. He told me that he had met with both final authorities and they had agreed to retain Cynthia subject to several modest conditions. A few days later I met with Cynthia to review the conditions. She gave me much more credit than I deserved for the good result. I told her that the man who was her ally believed in her and she deserved his confidence.

ॐ॰ ॐ॰ ॐ॰

# The "Gotcha" Client

STANLEY POLETSKY IS AN unusual client. A real estate developer from
Pennsylvania, Stanley does something clients rarely do. He reads the
lengthy documents I send him and he understands what he reads. In addition, Stanley asks questions about the documents. Ordinarily I would
enjoy a client who pays attention to what I do, but Stanley doesn't ask
questions to obtain information. He asks them to embarrass me. His
questions are meant as a challenge, to see whether he can show that I have
overlooked something.

A typical phone call from Stanley to my home at 10:45 p.m. explains
his method of operation. Stanley skips the verbal foreplay—there's no
"Hi, how are you?" or "Are you free to discuss the joint venture agreement?"—and goes straight to the main event. The main event goes like
this:

"Do you have a copy of the joint venture agreement?"

I'm tempted to say, "Sure, I'm sitting here with it by the phone waiting for your call." Instead I say, "I'll get it."

I return to the phone with a copy of the joint venture agreement.
"I've got it, Stanley, what's up?"

"I'm looking at page 34, the third full paragraph, lines 5 through 17.
My question is this: wouldn't those words bring about a burn-down even
if the joint venture's cash call was for funds to cure a defect in the consideration provided by either party for the joint venture itself? If it
becomes necessary to spend money to remove a cloud on the title of one
of the lots the Patterson group put in the joint venture in order to receive
its interest, this provision would seem to treat this as a cash call by the
joint venture. If our side failed to meet the cash call, our interest would
be subject to the burn-down. Am I reading it correctly?"

Fortunately, I can handle Stanley's gotcha this time. "No, you're not.
If the hypothetical situation you present should occur, there wouldn't be
a cash call by the joint venture. The joint venture would look solely to
the Patterson group for purchasing its interest with defective consideration. If you look at Section 9 on page 4, you'll see that it says the Patterson group is providing the lots to the joint venture 'in fee simple, with
warranties against all defects.' Under New York law a cloud on title is a
defect and the warranty would require the Pattersons to cure it or pay

damages to the joint venture in an amount sufficient to cure it. There's nothing to worry about in that situation."

Stanley was totally silent. He had lost the contest and knew it. If the question had been honest, Stanley would have thrown in the towel and thanked me for answering it. But Stanley isn't a good sport. He persists even when a match is over: "I see what you're saying, but wouldn't it be clearer if the wording on page 34 stated there will be no burn-down if the joint venture seeks cash from either party to remedy a defect in the consideration provided by that party? Don't you think so?"

I could have explained to Stanley why such additional words didn't make the situation any clearer. I could have explained why the joint venture couldn't make a cash call for such purpose under any circumstances. But with midnight approaching and no reason to do so, I decided not to drag the body around the ring: "No problem, Stanley, I'll put it in."

The phone call ended with one point for me and no points for Stanley. Nevertheless, Stanley's mock questions continued throughout the two and a half years it took to complete the work. Stanley was one of those clients willing to pay for a lawyer's time discussing things that might be better addressed by a psychiatrist.

ﳲﳲﳲ

# An Unsuccessful Musician

I HAVE A CLIENT who is a talented musician. His playing is considered by knowledgeable people to be almost—but not quite—as good as what are called world-class performers. In my profession if you have seventy-five percent you'll do very well and if you have ninety percent you'll get the golden ring. In music if you have ninety percent you'll get unemployment insurance. I think about this every time my musician client needs legal services. When things are going well for him, he'll make a few bucks playing at a restaurant, a wedding or other function, or in someone's home. When things are not going well, he can't afford his rent or food and must borrow money from friends, whom he is never able to repay.

This situation troubles me for several reasons. It troubles me that my client is unable to earn enough money to pay for his basic needs. It also troubles me that he has studied music and practiced his vocation as seriously as I have studied and practiced law. Who decided that a reasonably accomplished lawyer would be able to send his kids to private colleges and have a second home whereas a reasonably accomplished musician can't earn enough money to eat at a restaurant or go to a movie? I feel guilty asking "How's it going?" when I know with certainty it isn't going well. I have constructed an imaginary conversation with my client that makes me feel much better:

"How's it going?" I ask him.

"You won't believe it—I have terrific news for a change."

"Let me have it."

"I went to the trials for a seat in the New York Philharmonic. Shock of all shocks, I was selected! I begin next month, when the orchestra starts its new season."

"That's terrific! Did they give you a contract?"

"Yes. I think it's the standard union contract. Here's my copy. Please review it fast. How do you like the starting salary? That's more than I've made since I left the Conservatory."

I need flights of fantasy every once in awhile.

಼ಲ ಼ಲ ಼ಲ

# Questions in Annulment

STUART CARLTON WAS AN easy client to represent, easy, that is until he fell out of love with his wife and in love with a much younger woman living in another city. From what I could tell—we had dinner together with our wives on one occasion—Stuart had a good relationship with his wife. They had four children, ranging from their late teens to late twenties, and had sufficient money to be quite comfortable. Stuart's mid-life crisis, or whatever it should be called, put me in a difficult situation with him for the first time.

The first unwelcome request Stuart made to me was to tell anyone who inquired about his whereabouts, including his wife, that he was at a meeting he never attended. I told Stuart I was uneasy telling untruths on his behalf. When that failed to dissuade him, I told him he would almost surely be caught in the lie he was asking me to tell. The fictitious alibi scenario continued for several months. Although I secretly hoped Stuart would get caught, he never did.

The second disquieting matter that came to my attention involved money. Stuart wanted to put a substantial portion of his assets in accounts in his own name in banks that no one in his position would ever use. There was nothing illegal about the transfers themselves but they clearly took place in order to put a considerable portion of the Carltons' wealth where Stuart's wife couldn't find it. Since the money had been accumulated by the Carltons as a result of decades of cooperative efforts, I had serious reservations about what Stuart was doing. When I tried to discuss the matter with him he became irritated with me for the first time in our relationship: "I'll decide what to do with my money," Stuart told me, "she didn't earn one cent of it." Although the paychecks and dividends went to Stuart, not his wife, the money involved was attributable to efforts I knew Stuart's wife had made over many years. I almost asked him why, if he considered himself entitled to the money he was transferring, he didn't simply tell his wife what he was doing and skip the covert transfers. I restrained myself, but on reflection I wish I had not.

The last unpleasant matter I encountered concerning Stuart's new relationship was his effort to free himself from his marriage so that he could marry the other woman. Since Stuart and his wife were both devout Roman Catholics, there could not be a divorce. Stuart and his wife had to have their marriage annulled by authorities within the Church.

I had nothing to do with Stuart's separation and divorce, which involved an area of law I don't practice. One day, however, he made a request that I wish I had declined. He asked me to be available for an interview by the representative of the Church whose function it was to determine that Stuart's marriage had never been "consummated." Although I am certainly no expert in such matters, I thought "consummated" meant some combination of sexual intercourse and holding oneself out as married. Since the Carltons had four children and since Stuart and his wife had held themselves out as married for more than three decades, there was no question that these requirements were satisfied. My interview by the Church's representative disabused me of my understanding.

The interview took place by telephone. The man who conducted it never met me and never asked about any documents in my possession. Even more surprising, at no time during the interview did he ask anything about the matter of "consummation" as I understood it or in any other way. The interview was focused on only one subject: my opinion of Stuart's integrity as a client and as a business person. Stuart owned a business that served as a financial consultant to a wide range of clients. In these respects, Stuart's record was unblemished, and I told the interviewer so. He didn't ask me any specific questions regarding the matter of integrity and gave the impression of simply checking boxes in order to make an annulment possible.

I had imagined a somewhat different interview from what occurred. I asked the interviewer when he had finished whether he wanted to ask me anything about the matter of consummation. He did not. Had he wished to do so, I would have told him that to any outside party the Carltons' marriage seemed in every way to be a complete marriage, including four children.

᠔ ᠔ ᠔

# A Builder's Error

JOHN HENRY COSGROVE IS an old-fashioned builder and a good one. He's sullen, slow, assiduously attentive to detail, and honorable. John Henry does not come to me often. He does his own contracts and solves most of his legal problems himself. When he does come to me it is because something unusual has occurred.

John Henry was building a nice addition to a home in the country. The addition consisted of a large, carefully planned family room and a small bathroom. A new doorway from the existing house would open to the addition. As he often did, John Henry planned to do most of the work ordinarily done by subcontractors himself. He was planning to use subcontractors for the electrical and plumbing work only to the extent necessary to get the work approved.

The architect for the addition had prepared general plans and plans for each potential subcontractor. Because he was rushed to come up with a price for the work, John Henry reviewed only the general plans before making his bid. To price the portion of the electrical and plumbing work he himself would do, John Henry did what is known as a "takeoff" from the general plans. Takeoffs are usually performed by subcontractors, who are familiar with extracting the work required of their particular trades from general plans for projects.

John Henry's takeoff of the electrical work was not correct. He failed to take into account a considerable portion of the work required by the plans. As a result, John Henry's bid, which was accepted by the owners, a husband and wife, was unrealistically low. It was so low that by performing his contract at the price he set he would take a loss on the entire job.

John Henry came to my office more than a little embarrassed by his mistake, but, as always, totally forthright: "I blew it," he told me, "there's nothing else to say about it." After this admission, he asked me the question of the day: "Is there any legal way I can get out of doing the job at that price?" John Henry wasn't proud to be asking the question, and he looked at the floor as he did so.

The legal answer to John Henry's question was simple: he had entered into a contract and was required to perform it. The fact of his error had no legal consequences. I told him this, and he wasn't surprised to hear it. We sat silent, each of us thinking about how the problem might be addressed. I broke the silence:

"Look, John Henry, you made a mistake and that's it. You didn't do anything dishonest or unprofessional. Everyone makes mistakes. Why not simply go to the owners, tell them of your mistake, and ask whether they would consider letting you correct the price?"

The discussion with John Henry about my suggestion was difficult. He wanted to somehow correct his error—which would otherwise cost him about $17,000—but he didn't want to admit to the owners that he had made a mistake and ask them to forgive him for it. After much talk, we decided that I would contact one of the owners, probably the husband, and tell him what had happened. Depending on the response I received, I might be able to ask the owner to consider a price adjustment, even though he was not required to do so.

I saw the husband at his nearby downtown office and he was very gracious. He understood the mistake and why John Henry felt unable to come to him himself. He agreed to a price adjustment before the end of our conversation. When I told this to John Henry, he was very much relieved. He did a beautiful job on the addition.

è& è& è&

# A Risk Taker

I'VE KNOWN JOHN MADIGAN since he started his construction company fifteen years ago. John does almost everything right. He deals well with subcontractors, public agencies, and customers. He prices jobs carefully and makes appropriate contracts with customers. He purchases materials well and uses employees effectively.

One thing about John's business style that gives me reservations is that he is a far greater risk taker than I could be comfortable being. With John, I try to keep my risk aversion to myself. Sometimes I bite my tongue, but on rare occasions, I don't succeed.

For John, taking risks has paid off. He has undertaken difficult jobs that many similar contractors would not be willing to try to do. Often he has been able to outbid competitors by negotiating a chancy means of cost reduction with one or two prime subcontractors. John doesn't lose any sleep when he takes such risks. Because of this attitude, John's business has, in the fifteen years since he started out, grown from a one-man shop to a substantial construction company capable of large public and private jobs, sometimes costing millions of dollars.

On this occasion John's company had successfully bid on a very large public job and he has come to me to review the contract. Even before he leaves my office I see that the contractor is required by the contract to present what is known as a "payment and performance bond." Such a bond assures the owner, in this instance the State of Maryland, that the contractor will pay all suppliers and subcontractors in full before a lien is placed on the property and also that the contractor will complete the job in accordance with its specifications. On public jobs bonds such as this one are issued by large bonding companies that require the principal owners of the contractor and their spouses to guarantee them.

If something goes wrong and the bonding company is called on to pay money, the guarantors are responsible for reimbursing it. If John's company fails to pay all the material suppliers and subcontractors or if it fails to complete the job successfully, John and his wife will be liable to the bonding company for a considerable amount of money. In fact, the Madigans could owe the bonding company more than their net worth. John is doing what is known as "betting the ranch" on the satisfactory and profitable completion of the work required by the contract.

John asked me to explain to him all the risks presented by this undertaking, but not to advise him whether to accept them. I'm the lawyer, and
John is the businessman. I try unsuccessfully to keep my thoughts to
myself, but before John leaves my office, I cannot hold back any longer:

> You can see, John, that this contract requires a payment and perform-
> ance bond guaranteed by you and Harriet. If you enter the contract,
> you will be risking your entire net worth. We're talking about the
> house, the kids' college, retirement—everything. You've worked very
> hard, John, and you're in excellent financial shape. Does it make sense
> to risk everything for the possible profit this job would give you if all
> goes well?

John quickly digests what I am saying, and I can see by his expression that my gratuitous advice will not be taken. "This job is a slam-
dunk," he tells me, "it's big but it's not complicated. We've done lots of
jobs that were far more difficult." I'm sure what John is saying is true, but
it doesn't change my opinion. If things go wrong, even something that
no one could imagine, John's financial security is gone. This job is so big
that even a relatively minor snag could cost the bonding company, and
hence John and Harriet, more money than they have accumulated over
fifteen years of hard work.

To make my point as strongly as possible, I tell John about a disastrous
situation that another contractor faced. I exaggerate the harm the other
contractor suffered, and I fail to mention that the other job was not a simple one. I have dealt with construction contracts of extreme simplicity
where an unforeseen condition, such as unknown rock beneath the surface where a foundation was to go, cost the bonding company, and hence
the guarantors, more money than the whole job was worth. This is the
best I can do to persuade John not to take this risk, but even before I finish speaking I see I have failed.

For each hypothetical fact I add to the story, John comes up with an
explanation for why it is not convincing. He's like a patient who won't
stop questioning the doctor until a favorable diagnosis is given. Our
meeting ends with a suggestion I am certain John will not take: "Discuss
it with Harriet, John, before you make your decision." I realize, as John
gets up and heads for the door, that practicing law is much harder when
you care about clients.

Fortunately, John's construction company completes the job with no
difficulty and makes a handsome profit.

ểầ  ểầ  ểầ

# Husband with Two Marriages

ONE MORNING JUST AFTER I arrived at the office I received a phone call
from a man named Floyd Harding. I had heard of Floyd, but had never
met or talked with him. He got right to the point: "I need to see you as
soon as possible. I can't discuss this on the phone."

Whenever I receive such calls they always mean one of two things:
the caller is being investigated or prosecuted for a crime or the caller has
just been sued in a serious case such as professional malpractice or fraud.
Neither proved to be Floyd's situation.

I made an appointment with Floyd for three o'clock that day and he
arrived at two-thirty. Floyd was older than I had imagined and looked
every one of his 60-plus years. His clothes were expensive, but they were
badly pressed and could have used a good cleaning. Floyd sat down in the
chair to which I motioned, declined my offer of a cup of coffee, and
started right in:

"I have two marriages. One is a legal marriage and I have two children with that wife. The other is a marriage in every way except a license.
My second wife is legally married to her husband, but he travels a lot.
We've got an apartment in Annapolis and I gave her a car she keeps there.
She uses one of my credit cards, but the bills come to the office. We travel
and go out as a married couple, so there are people who know what's
what."

Covert relationships of married people are certainly not unusual, but
a second marriage is something else. That Floyd and his second wife were
able to accomplish this amazed me. "How long has this gone on?" I asked.
"It's gone on a little over ten years," Floyd replied. "My wife found out
when someone saw us and told her. She found out years ago, but I prom-
ised her then that it was over and we got by it. This time she got a lawyer
and she wants to cut off my you-know-what."

"What about your second wife, does her husband know?"

"I don't know, but if he doesn't, he will soon."

A few days later I met with Floyd and his second wife. To my surprise, given Floyd's appearance, she was at most 30 years old. She confirmed everything Floyd had told me. I advised her that she needed her
own lawyer and it couldn't be me. I referred her to a friend of mine, who
saw her within the next two days. "She's really young," my friend told me

after he had met with her, "and it's quite a story. Do you believe they've pulled this off for more than ten years?"

The rest of the story proved to be as surprising as the first part: After a few months, my client's first wife told her lawyer she didn't want to proceed any further. She had made up her mind to do nothing, provided she could continue to live in their sumptuous house and receive the same monthly allowance she had been receiving. The second wife's husband did nothing whatsoever, and we never found out whether he knew of his wife's other relationship and chose to accept it or, unlikely as it was, didn't know about it.

My friend and I told our respective clients that the relationship presented serious risks of legal difficulties, such as charges of adultery or even bigamy. We told them that they should discontinue their relationship. My client told me he would consider the advice.

I ran across my client several years later while attending a concert with my wife. He was there with his first wife and his second wife was there with her husband. Seeing each of them with their legal spouses was a strange sight. Apparently, my client had continued his relationship with his second wife. At intermission. he sidled over to me and asked whether I thought it was better for him to register the car he had purchased for his second wife in his own name. Floyd was concerned that someone might learn the car was registered to his second wife and wonder why she kept it in an Annapolis garage.

za za za

# An Astounding Income

A NEW CLIENT WHO had a small crew of men working for him to repair HVAC systems came to see me. From his appearance—soiled khaki pants, a frayed pullover shirt covered with plaster dust and work boots—it was clear that he participated in the physical labor. Given the nature of his work, I assumed he earned a modest income.

The matter for which he had come to me was relatively simple. It concerned a contract with the owners of an office building. The form contract he handed me had clearly not been prepared by a lawyer. Since my client's matter had tax implications, I asked him to provide me with copies of his federal income tax returns for the past two years. From looking at them I would be able to address a significant part of his concern. Everything suggested I should economize to the fullest possible extent on time and expense.

The matter of concern to my client was easily resolved and I saw him only one more time, when he brought his tax returns with him. I looked them over briefly while he was in my office. The tax return for two years ago showed a taxable income of about $1.2 million. The tax return for the past year showed a taxable income of about $1.4 million. I was stunned. "I guess you do all right," I said. He answered with no special affect, "I guess so."

ॐ ॐ ॐ

# A Terrible Injury

ONE OF THE SADDEST cases I ever had involved a young woman who was physically and mentally challenged. The facts were simple: my client, Evelyn Burchley, went to a chiropractor for relief of pain in her neck. Although the chiropractor was aware of Evelyn's disabilities and knew he was supposed to bill her mother, he inadvertently sent his bill directly to Evelyn. The bill went unpaid and was ultimately referred by the chiropractor to a collection agency.

The collection agency hounded Evelyn mercilessly, finally telling her that if she did not pay the bill promptly, she would be arrested and put in jail. Evelyn went to a nearby office building, walked up to the fourth floor, and jumped out a window in an attempt to kill herself. Amazingly, she did not die from the fall, even though the description of her body on the sidewalk provided by the police officer called to the scene was horrifying.

I instituted a lawsuit on Evelyn's behalf against both the chiropractor and the collection agency. Our case was strong because our investigation had disclosed violations of both state and federal bill collection laws. Evelyn waited outside the courtroom most of the time and did not testify. I believe she did not understand what was occurring. After short deliberations, the jury awarded Evelyn a substantial sum of money.

After the verdict, for reasons unrelated to the conduct of either lawyer, the court declared a mistrial. Evelyn's case had to be retried. Because I have an intense dislike of retrials, I asked one of my partners to handle the retrial. He did and, to our disbelief, won precisely the same amount of damages that Evelyn had been awarded in the first trial. The money was placed in a trust controlled by her guardians.

Evelyn had no idea that she had received the money. She left the courthouse without any conversation and neither my partner nor I ever heard from her or her family thereafter. It's unusual for lawyers to recover a substantial sum of money for a client who is unaware of what occurred. When, after two successful trials, we closed Evelyn's file, there was no reason to write her a final letter.

ả ả ả

# Clients' Expectations

A FRIEND IN THE advertising business tells me the following: "The hardest client for me is the one who believes he makes a good product and offers it at a bargain price. The client I like says, 'I wrap dog droppings in leaves and want to sell them as a gourmet food item.' This guy knows he doesn't deserve anything and he's grateful for whatever he gets."

My friend's cynicism is certainly not a generous comment about the advertising business, but there's some truth in it for my business as well. A client who believes he deserves everything is a difficult client to satisfy. If you accomplish everything any lawyer could hope to accomplish, your client believes he simply received what he deserved. If you accomplish 90% of everything possible, your client may wonder whether he might have received 100% with another lawyer. The short way of saying this is that big expectations lead to big disappointments.

I have both kinds of clients. One of my clients is a "trust fund baby" who has never worked a day in his life. He's president of one of his family's businesses, but someone else makes the important decisions. This guy likes to pretend he's exceptionally detail oriented. He does this at my expense by expressing reservations about details of my work about which he knows nothing. I tolerate him because the business pays his bills and what he is doing is harmless.

Another client cuts every corner imaginable and freely admits that he gets away with murder. I advise him when he gets too close to the edge and he jokingly thanks me for doing so. This guy makes no pretense of deserving anything. He considers himself lucky not to get caught most of the time. He knows he's skating on the edge and all he expects from his lawyer is whatever help I can give him. This guy is the easy client, of course.

Every lawyer takes clients as they come.

ॐ  ॐ  ॐ

# Immoral Client

HERMAN CORDOVAN WAS ONE of those clients with no moral bearings whatsoever. Herman was a banker who owned a substantial interest in the bank and served it as its executive vice president. He didn't recognize having any responsibility to anyone other than himself and the other owners of the bank. Every decision Herman made on behalf of the bank was based on whatever most benefited him and the other owners.

Although Herman's behavior was deplorable, it did not make him a difficult client. What made him a difficult client was his failure to imagine any possible objections to his actions. Herman believed that whatever benefited him was right and just. He was a middle-aged man with an infant's sense of entitlement. Any effort to suggest—and I made many efforts—that the interests of others might deserve recognition was futile. On more than one occasion, Herman said outright that he couldn't understand why people had a problem with his agenda.

Not surprisingly, Herman got into trouble because of his blindness to the effect of his actions on others. The deals he had made on behalf of his bank had frequently resulted in financial damage to depositors and borrowers. Herman's business conduct eventually came to the attention of law enforcement authorities and criminal charges were made against him. This led to his loss of authority to act on behalf of the bank.

Herman's wrongful conduct was easily provable, and the only possibly beneficial course of action was to engage in plea bargaining. I did so, going back and forth between the prosecutor and Herman with various proposals. Herman's self-absorption impeded the process. When the prosecutor made a point concerning the adverse effect of Herman's conduct on others, I would make an effort to discuss it with Herman to determine whether there were any mitigating factors. But that proved impossible. Herman was incapable of seeing that something beneficial to him might not be desirable or similarly beneficial to others.

When I referred to his misdeeds, Herman would give me a blank, uncomprehending stare without realizing why others didn't understand his decision the way he did. For all intents and purposes, I had no client to involve in the plea bargaining process, so I was forced to fashion justifications for Herman's conduct from whatever facts I was able to garner without his assistance. There was no possibility of accomplishing anything for Herman on the basis of his skewed view of his business practices. I constructed Herman's arguments to the prosecutor as I would have had he been either insane or dead.

The most difficult part of the situation was avoiding making arguments to the prosecutor that might suggest Herman's moral bankruptcy. I was forced to make mitigating arguments as though Herman was saying things that supported such arguments. Candor prevented me from ascribing my arguments to Herman. This proved awkward, to say the least, and I wouldn't be surprised if the prosecutor had inferred that Herman was unable to make a case for himself.

Ultimately, the prosecutor and I agreed on a plea bargain. The plea bargain was neither as bad as it might have been for Herman nor as good as I would have liked. I had only a few discussions with Herman after he agreed to the language of the written plea bargain. In these discussions it was clear to me that Herman felt I had let him down. His question was, "Why should a man who hasn't done anything wrong pay any penalty whatsoever?" By then I knew it wasn't worth trying to suggest that other people disagreed with him.

 è. è. è.

# Holocaust Survivor

MY CLIENT AND FIVE other men were charged with the crime of price fixing. The defendants had agreed to take turns obtaining state contracts at vastly inflated prices. The understanding was that each time bids were accepted for a contract an agreed-upon member of the group would submit the winning bid. The other companies would submit higher bids. The winning bid was always much higher than it would have been had the bidding been competitive. Although the prosecutor's case was close to a slam dunk, all the defendants rejected plea possibilities and chose instead to go to trial. A date for trial was set by the court as soon as preliminary matters were addressed.

Of the six defendants, my client was the only one to be offered the opportunity to receive a recommendation from the prosecutor of no incarceration if he would provide information about the group's agreement and testify as a prosecution witness. Although there was no guarantee that the court would accept the prosecution's recommendation, the history of such agreements was that the court probably would accept it. The prosecutor approached me with the possible deal a month or so before the scheduled trial. Without a deal, my client would almost certainly receive a sentence that included substantial incarceration.

The plea bargain offered was one that would ordinarily be irresistible. I recommended acceptance to my client and expected his reasonably prompt agreement. To my surprise, he instantly rejected the plea bargain without explanation. I had never known a client to do this.

In the hope he might reconsider the offer after giving it further thought and discussing it with his wife, I didn't immediately tell the prosecutor of my client's response. After nearly a week I scheduled a meeting with my client to discuss the prosecutor's offer again. When I raised the subject, his response was identical: he didn't want to discuss it. I asked why he wouldn't at least consider the offer, and his answer was one with which no one could argue.

My client explained that he had been in Buchenwald during the Holocaust and that every member of his extended family had been sent to the gas chambers. He showed me a booklet listing among the honored dead more than twenty people with his last name. He told me that during the Holocaust many of those exterminated had been turned over to the Nazis by informants. He said that providing information to the government about other people was unacceptable to him and beyond discussion.

My client and I never discussed the possible plea bargain again. The prosecutor could barely believe me when I told him that his offer had been declined. My client went to trial with the other defendants and all were convicted and sentenced to terms of incarceration. After unsuccessful appeals they all began serving their sentences. Several months later the prosecutor agreed to release of my client for health reasons. I had previously told the prosecutor, in confidence, of my client's experience during the Holocaust. I came to believe the prosecutor was looking for a justification for releasing my client from incarceration.*

---

*I have had only one other case in which the Holocaust affected the outcome. It was a case that involved the division of money owned jointly by my client and her wife-beating ex-husband. A creditor had attached the jointly-owned fund. In any other situation, the creditor would have been legally entitled to the entire fund. When, however, I advised the court that my client's contribution to the fund consisted of money she had received from her father, who had received it from the German government as reparation for what he experienced at the hands of the Nazis, the judge took the very unusual step of dividing the fund and ordering my client's share to be paid to her.

ża ża ża

# A Difficult Client

EARLY IN MY PRACTICE I was advised never to accept a client who had previously used more than one lawyer in a particular case. In most instances, I followed that advice, but on one occasion I disregarded it and I paid for doing so.

My client was a builder who had a bad reputation for not getting along with others. There were people who said they would never deal with him again. The person who introduced us, however, had dealt with my client agreeably on numerous occasions. I thought I would be able to do that too, but I didn't know that my client had a strong motive for getting along with the man who had referred him to me. Because he had no such motive to do so with me, his conduct became consistent with his reputation.

The first sign of trouble was my client's concern about small items on bills. "Why did you need to go see the Evans site?" he asked on one occasion. On another he said, "You spoke with the contractor's lawyer five times last month. What could you possibly have talked about?" For a while my answers to such questions appeared to be satisfactory, but soon my client's attitude changed. Within a few weeks, it was clear he would quibble about every item on every bill. Initially his remarks simply suggested I was inefficient, but then he began to challenge my integrity and competence. I realized that my client didn't intend to pay his bills under any circumstances.

The second phase of his attack was the suggestion that I had a conflict of interest and wasn't representing him vigorously. He never made the nature of the conflict of interest clear, but he would make remarks such as, "You can't deal with both sides of a contract. I thought you were going to work for me exclusively." When I asked him to whom else I was showing loyalty, he said, "You know full well what I'm talking about." I didn't have the slightest idea what he was talking about and, I suspect, neither did he.

Eventually I escaped my client's grasp with only an unpaid bill to show for it. He even telephoned me once to say there were no hard feelings. This client's conduct was not unique. Many clients use spurious allegations against those who work for them to escape payment for services.

I was surprised by something I learned shortly after my relationship with this client ended. I learned that he had a good deal of integrity when it came to his buildings. He went to considerable lengths to avoid cutting down trees unnecessarily. He used 2X6 studding when 2X4 studding would have satisfied building code requirements. He used solid hardware when hollow hardware would have sufficed. And he made his buildings architecturally significant even when square boxes would have served the purpose. It is interesting to me that a client with no integrity whatsoever regarding dealings with others had considerable integrity regarding the buildings he constructed.

☙ ☙ ☙

# An Incompetent Son

THE SON OF A wealthy and successful businessman phoned me one morning: "I have to see you immediately, " he said, "I'm bringing Janice with me." My client wouldn't call in this manner unless the matter was urgent. I told him I'd see him later that morning.

When he and his wife arrived it was immediately clear that he was embarrassed and she was angry. "Tell him what happened," she said, taking a seat on the other side of the table from her husband. He hesitated and I saw that his eyes were red, presumably from crying. His wife glowered at him as if to say, "Get on with it."

His story was not a happy one. He had been running a small, unsuccessful business with two partners. For years he had extracted money from a family trust he was supposed to manage for himself and his siblings and using the money to keep the unsuccessful business afloat. The business could not be made profitable and my client was ashamed of having failed. "It all started with a few hundred dollars a month, then it became thousands and kept growing," my client stammered, "and now there's no way I can pay it all back." His wife's expression was a mixture of anger and disgust.

Since the matter concerned my client's family, which I was sure would not sue him, I advised him to tell his siblings what he had done. His older sister, who had always thought him incompetent to run a business, would be furious, and none of them would be surprised to learn he had extracted money from their trust. My client knew what they would think of him. His wife agreed with my recommendation that he speak to his siblings immediately. It was clear from her demeanor that she'd had enough of him. I said a few things about the legal steps necessary to close the business and the meeting ended on a solemn note.

As they got up to leave, my client lagged behind. "Do you think I'll have to get out of the country club?" he asked, looking deeply into my eyes. I couldn't believe what I was hearing and was unable to contain myself: "Do you really think that's important right now?"

A few weeks later I learned from a divorce lawyer with whom I was acquainted that my client had engaged her to represent him with respect to the divorce complaint his wife had brought against him. This came as no surprise. I never heard from this client again, but months afterward his wife called me to let me know their divorce had become final.

*ea ea ea*

# Mistaken Belief in Client

MY CLIENT, LYDIA BURKHART, was involved in a long and unpleasant lawsuit against a man who had employed her for many years. Lydia alleged various forms of discrimination as well as nonpayment of commissions she had earned. Her employer alleged her failure to perform her duties in accordance with her employment contract and divulgence of confidential information to outsiders. I believed in my client's position and made that clear to the lawyer representing her employer. For a long time he said nothing about my opinion and I assumed his silence indicated that, however reluctantly, he had accepted it.

One day my adversary, a competent and honest lawyer with whom I had dealt previously, surprised me when I repeated that I believed my client's position. His remark was something like "I know you believe what your client is telling you, but I'm telling you she's an absolute liar. I've spent a lot of time speaking with folks who work with her and you have no way to reach them. If you knew what they're saying, your opinion of your client's veracity would be totally different."

As a result of my colleague's remark, I questioned my client more vigorously than I had previously. Under additional pressure her story began to vary and, ultimately, she flatly contradicted herself. I was embarrassed to have to admit to my colleague, in confidence, that my belief regarding my client's position had changed.

❦ ❦ ❦

# Sexual Misconduct

I HAD A CLIENT who couldn't keep his hands, much less his eyes, off women's breasts and crotches. My client often wound up with one of his hands in precisely the wrong place. He would pretend to be reaching for something on the other side of a woman when it was obvious that his intention was otherwise. Women in his office, to whom this occurred repeatedly, spoke to an officer of the company about my client's conduct, and the officer ultimately spoke to me. When I discussed the matter with my client it was clear to me that he knew exactly what I was talking about but pretended to be surprised. "I never had any such intention," he protested with transparent conviction.

I suggested that he see someone professional about his difficulty. He was offended by the suggestion and never followed it. Then I suggested that he establish some ground rules to avoid future misunderstandings. Among the ground rules was leaving his office door open at all times when a woman was in it, taking a third party to lunches and other occasions when a woman was involved, and avoiding taking women in his car. My client felt that these precautions were unnecessary, but he accepted them to avoid future misunderstandings. I mistakenly thought the problem was solved.

One day my client phoned me from a police station in a part of the state where a senior executive such as he was wouldn't ordinarily be found. He explained that he had been arrested several blocks from a nightclub frequented by prostitutes. A policeman had observed him receiving oral sex from a prostitute in his car, a brand-new Mercedes. Standard tests had shown that my client was very drunk at the time.

I had no experience with such cases and asked my partner, a former state prosecutor, if she would take the case. She agreed, met with my client, and negotiated a plea bargain with the state prosecutor. My client was fined, placed on probation, and given the opportunity to have his record cleared after a year of successful probation. Remarkably, my client's desire to have the case concluded without his wife learning what occurred was satisfied.

A while later I asked my client what could possibly have enticed him into such a situation. Since he appeared to have a good relationship with his wife, who was gorgeous, the risks he took seemed not to be justified solely by sexual desire. My client explained that he had just completed a very important job and had gone to the prostitute-ridden nightclub "to celebrate." He said that the prostitute with whom he was arrested had picked him up on his way out and admitted he was intoxicated. To me, his explanation lacked credibility. He had risked physical injury, arrest, and disease, not to mention extreme embarrassment, for what he did. I've never figured out what was going on in his mind.

ᨆ ᨆ ᨆ

# Just a Mistake

EARLY ONE SATURDAY MORNING before the weekend receptionist arrived, the phone rang in my office. I answered it, only to be surprised by the caller's bluntness: "I need you to help my son. He's sixteen. He has to go to court. It's all a mistake." Clarence Flossbein, who I later learned was a supplier of slipcovers and curtains that he installed in people's homes, didn't give his name or explain who had referred him to me. He didn't even explain the difficulty concerning his son.

When Clarence and his son arrived the following Monday, I could see that they wished they didn't have to talk about the matter. My attempts to exchange a few pleasantries to break the ice failed completely. Clarence, a short, restrained man with a foreign accent, spoke as though every word caused him great pain. "This is Donald, my son. What happened was all a mistake," he said as he handed me a summons requiring Donald to appear in court for two misdemeanor charges. The charges related to misconduct of a sexual nature in a public place. Donald's face was ashen and he appeared catatonic, sitting motionless with his eyes toward the floor as I read the summons. I told Clarence I wanted to speak with Donald alone and he left immediately for the waiting room.

The next twenty minutes would surely be among the worst experiences in Donald's life. I had to ask a long series of questions in order to elicit what had occurred. To each of them Donald provided the least possible information. While we spoke, he never looked at me nor was there any change in the flatness of his voice. The story he told, robot-like, was fairly simple but greatly humiliating.

Donald had been arrested by an undercover policeman while seeking to procure oral sex in the men's room of a light rail station not far from his house. As with every offender caught committing a humiliating offense, Donald claimed he had not intended to do anything and that it was all a mistake. He also said, as such offenders frequently do, that it was "the only time this had happened." The police officer had taken Donald to the police station and subsequently to appear before a magistrate who explained the charges to him, set a date for a court appearance, and then released him into his father's custody. In his first show of emotion, Donald implored me not to tell his father what he had just told me.

I invited Clarence back into my office and I complied with Donald's request. As Clarence and I talked, I learned that his wife, with whom he had two children—Donald and an older sister in her first year of nursing school—had not been told why Donald had been arrested. He said, falsely as I later learned, that she was very ill and therefore unable to deal with the situation.

By the time Clarence and his son left my office it was clear that complete suppression of what had occurred was of the greatest importance to them. "It was a mistake," was the mantra I repeatedly heard from both father and son. This concluded the first and only meeting I had with either of them. There was no discussion of how I would proceed, what my fee would be, or anything else. I rarely ended a first meeting with a client without discussing these matters.

The court date for Donald's case was set for about six weeks later. I wanted to meet with the undercover officer before then. I also wanted to meet with the state's attorney prosecuting the case. This meeting would have to take place close to the trial date because state's attorneys for minor offenses are assigned just before trial.

When I telephoned the police station to which the undercover officer was assigned, I was surprised to find that he was in and would take my call. Officer Brad Williams agreed to meet me at the station the next day. It is because of his decency and compassion that what Donald and his father devoutly hoped for, that is, absolute confidentiality, did indeed occur. A lawyer cannot manufacture generosity and Officer Williams's generosity made it possible for the Flossbein family to survive what happened.

When I met with Officer Williams I learned he had graduated from the police academy only a month before he arrested Donald. His first assignment was to serve undercover in the men's room at the light rail station where numerous encounters like the one Donald was charged with had been the cause of complaints to the local police. Brad and I quickly developed a friendly relationship, and he told me that his two-week stint in the men's room was "so disgusting" that he had seriously considered leaving the force. He had made nine arrests, eight adult men and Donald. The adults included two successful businessmen, one successful professional man, and the rest were successful in other fields of work. All but two were married and five were fathers. Brad was amazed that men of such standing would go to a public men's room seeking sexual encounters with strangers.

Although I checked repeatedly during the following weeks, it was not until the week before Donald's court date that I learned which judge would be presiding and which state's attorney would be prosecuting Donald. The state's attorney was David Foster, an overworked man who had been in that position for five or six years. When I told him the purpose of my phone call, he immediately put my call on hold. When he returned to the phone he cut to the chase: "Assuming your client has no priors, he could plead to either of the counts—you pick it—and I won't argue with P.B.J." (Probation before Judgment). This was the result I had hoped for. In Maryland a sentence of P.B.J. entitles a defendant, if the probation is satisfactory, to have the record fully expunged. I would have preferred to have the state's attorney agree to affirmatively recommend P.B.J., but not resisting it was good enough.

Things had worked out well with both the arresting officer and the state's attorney, but the judge was another story. Judge Harold Hogarth had a reputation for being unsympathetic toward defendants and, from all I learned about him, he was expected to regard Donald's conduct with particular distaste. Since judges in lower state courts decide cases without juries, Judge Hogarth alone would determine whether Donald was guilty and, if so, what his sentence would be. I heard from several colleagues that, other than to veterans of Vietnam, the judge rarely, if ever, showed a defendant mercy. One of my colleagues said, "If you can get P.B.J. out of that guy, you've hit a home run. Good luck!"

This portrait of Judge Hogarth presented me with a dilemma. On the one hand, I wanted Donald's case to come to trial before the judge who handled the other eight light rail men's room cases. I thought the contrast between a fifteen-year-old boy and eight established, successful men would be in Donald's favor. On the other hand, it was possible that, if I requested and obtained a delay, a more lenient judge might be chosen to hear Donald's case. Ultimately, I opted for the first alternative. Concluding the case as quickly as possible was highly desirable.

On the day of trial I asked Clarence and Donald to meet me in front of the courthouse one hour ahead of the scheduled time. Normally I would have met with a client the day before trial, but the prospect of another conversation with father or son about the case was so agonizing for them that I didn't arrange a meeting. The weather was warm, and I chose a bench near the courthouse as the place for us to confer.

Exactly on time Clarence and Donald arrived dressed in dark suits and neckties and black shoes, as if for a funeral. Clarence spoke very little, but enough to let me know that the "mistake" mantra was still fixed in his mind. Donald spoke not at all. I explained generally how the proceeding would go, making the state's attorney's statement of facts sound as inoffensive as I could. I was aware that hearing that statement of facts would destroy Clarence's "mistake" hypothesis and further humiliate Donald before his father.

When I saw Brad approaching the courthouse I told Clarence and Donald to remain seated and walked over to talk to him. He and I shook hands as if we were friends, which emboldened me to begin with the word "we" instead of "I": "We have to somehow get this done without Donald's father hearing the statement of facts and without Donald's having to agree to them in front of a packed courtroom." Brad's response reminded me that there are little pockets of kindness in the callous and confused system of criminal justice: "How can *we* do that?" he responded without hesitation.

My plan was to go to Judge Hogarth's chambers before he would come to the bench to hear the morning cases. All the men's room cases, including Donald's, were scheduled to be heard in sequence early in the morning cases. If I could see Judge Hogarth in his chambers, I could request that Donald's case be heard at a separate time, preferably when almost everyone in the courtroom had left for lunch. I hoped that the state's attorney and Brad would join me in this request. If Judge Hogarth agreed to it, I would take Clarence out of the courtroom before Donald was arraigned, direct him to a bench away from the courtroom door, and tell him to sit there until I returned. I knew that Clarence would obey these instructions.

Having seated my client and his father, I got into Judge Hogarth's chambers with the state's attorney and Brad only a few minutes before the judge was to head to the courtroom. As best I could, I explained why the case of a fifteen-year-old boy was different from the cases of adult men. I told Judge Hogarth a little about Donald's family and that I had arranged for his father to remain outside the courtroom. As I spoke, from a standing position since the judge had not invited us to sit, I could see hostility and indifference in his expression.

I could not have persuaded Judge Hogarth to do anything had it not been for Brad's intervention: "Judge, I made the arrests in all these cases and this one was the hardest. The others were well-established men and this kid isn't even sixteen. I have no idea why he got involved in this stuff, but I know that if he were my son I would pray that he got another chance. I'm asking you to do what Donald's lawyer is requesting." On only a few occasions have I seen a law enforcement officer responsible for a case act as compassionately as Brad did in saying this. Judge Hogarth's response left no doubt who had won the day for Donald: "Well, if that's what you want, we'll do it."

A few minutes after noon, Judge Hogarth had finished all but one case on the morning schedule. I had followed the progress of these cases carefully, in order to arrange for Donald's case to be heard when the courtroom was as empty as possible. While Judge Hogarth was hearing the last case, I walked to the last row of seats in the courtroom, where Clarence and Donald sat, and asked Clarence to follow me outside. In the hallway, I led him to the bench farthest from the courtroom door and motioned him to sit down. Briefly, implying that the instructions as to where he should remain came from elsewhere, I said, "Clarence, you have to sit here until I return. It's going to be a little while." There are very few situations in which a lawyer can justify lying. I believe this was one of them.

As I reentered the courtroom, the clerk called the Donald Flossbein case. I spoke immediately and as quickly as I felt would be acceptable to Judge Hogarth: "Your Honor, Mr. Flossbein wishes to enter a guilty plea to Count 1 of the information. Mr. Foster will advise you of the terms of the plea agreement. Mr. Flossbein understands the charges against him, and has had the opportunity to consult with me. He enters this plea voluntarily and without coercion and is prepared to be sentenced today." Judge Hogarth, adhering to the script, spoke next: "Mr. Foster, please state the terms of the plea agreement." The state's attorney then told the court he had agreed to dismiss Count 2 and not resist my recommendation of a sentence of P.B.J.

The judge then spoke: "Mr. Flossbein, do you understand what your attorney and the state's attorney have stated?" Donald quietly said yes. Judge Hogarth then requested the state's attorney to state the facts of the case. Donald looked down at his feet as a nearly empty courtroom was told that an undercover policeman, Officer Brad Williams, present in court, had seen Donald in a stall of the men's room at the Owings Mills light rail station gesturing to his exposed penis while a man in an adjoining stall observed him through a crack in the partition. Judge Hogarth then asked Donald what may well be the hardest question he would ever answer: "Mr. Flossbein, do you understand the facts the state's attorney has proffered and, understanding them, admit that they are correct?" I leaned over and told Donald he should say, "Yes, Your Honor, I understand." Donald never looked up from his feet as he complied.

Leaving the courtroom, I thanked Brad and the state's attorney for their cooperation in the case. I wanted to say a good deal more to Brad, but I saw Clarence looking very anxious as he sat on the distant bench. "Clarence," I said, "it's all finished. No conviction was placed on Donald's record and in two years the record will be expunged. Nothing is going to happen."

Had I been a witness in a judicial proceeding, what I said to Clarence would have been the truth and nothing but the truth but it would not have been the whole truth. The whole truth, particularly the truth about what Donald had admitted in court, would have completely destroyed Clarence's tightly held notion of a "mistake" and it would have let Donald know that his father understood precisely what he had done. When Clarence's eyes filled with tears and he turned away so that I would not notice, I knew it had been right to remove him from the courtroom.

≈ ≈ ≈

# Meat Pricing Conspiracy

THE MORNING NEWS STATED that criminal charges had been instituted against a group of meat suppliers. The group included some of the largest suppliers of meat in the country and one small local supplier. My partners and I were reasonably sure that at least one of the companies charged would come to our law firm for representation. As it turned out, the small local supplier was the one that became our client. We agreed to represent this company even though doing so meant we couldn't represent one of the large suppliers.

Our client was owned by a stocky, compact man in his late sixties who made it clear from the outset that he had little regard for lawyers. One manifestation of his attitude was his reluctance to pay our bills. When, at the conclusion of our first meeting, we came to the subject of legal fees he said, "Don't be one of those guys who keeps the clock running when you go to the bathroom."

To make the situation more difficult, each of the large national suppliers had several lawyers from large law firms. Together with assistants and assistants to the assistants, each court hearing looked like a wedding reception and took an inordinate amount of time. Soon the owner of the small meat supplier began to question every expenditure of time I made in the case. "Do you need to answer all these motions?" he would ask me, or "You don't need to become a meat expert to handle this case, do you?" Similar remarks persisted throughout our dealings.

I needed to learn how my client operated in order to defend it properly. The owner became highly antagonistic: "You're gonna bill me to look at frozen meat? How about I send you a photograph?" When he realized that indeed I was going to visit the business, he used another tack. "You're gonna have to get over at five in the morning to see what goes on when the trucks are loading. If you stay in the freezer, I'll tell you right now you're gonna freeze your ass off." There was no point in arguing and I said simply, "I'll be there at five on Thursday morning and I'll be wearing two sweaters and two pairs of gloves."

When I arrived on Thursday the owner and I entered the freezer immediately. In it there were sides of frozen meat of the sort referred to by the prosecutor throughout the hearings. "You seen enough?" the owner asked me as a U-Haul truck was backing up to the loading platform outside the freezer. A workman cut the sides in half and both pieces were placed in the truck. "We're not Safeway or A&P with big trucks," the owner said, "we sell independent markets that buy halves of sides and our trucks are too small for the whole ones."

The punch line of this story is that on the basis of what I learned in the freezer, I was able to convince the prosecutor that the local supplier wasn't a competitor of the national suppliers. The information about cutting the sides of meat, small trucks, and independent markets convinced him. Our client was dismissed from the case before trial, avoiding almost certain conviction, a large fine, and much higher legal fees. When I told the owner of the dismissal of his company, he made the only kind remark I ever heard from him: "You done OK for us. If we ever get into trouble again I got your number."*

---

*My description of this incident might suggest I believed the owner didn't like or trust me. That is not so. Despite his gruffness, I believe he did like and trust me and, I realized one morning in the coldest place I have ever been, I liked him as well.

ท่า ท่า ท่า

# Representing a Large Bank

LATE ONE AFTERNOON I received a phone call from Hargrove Sutley, assistant general counsel of a large New York bank. I had never served that bank, and Hargrove didn't tell me how he was referred to me. He asked if I could handle a case against the bank in federal court in Baltimore. It was a garden-variety case for a commercial bank, in which the bank and the borrower each contended that the other had breached the loan agreement. The amount involved was a few hundred thousand dollars, small potatoes for a large New York bank. When I told Hargrove I could handle the case, he said he would e-mail me the complaint and some other "stuff." Just before he hung up, he said "Send your bills to my attention." He never asked about my billing practices.

Although the call was brief, I detected an undercurrent of annoyance in Hargrove's voice. I assumed this tone was due either to another matter or to Hargrove's displeasure with having to deal with an outside lawyer. Checking the lawyer's directory, I learned that Hargrove was a graduate of a prestigious law school and that he had held his position at the bank for five years. I also learned that he had never represented a real live client at a trial of any kind.

I received the complaint, loan agreement and some correspondence from Hargrove the next morning. I knew within the first fifteen minutes what my strategy in the case would be. I knew I would file a counterclaim against the borrower who had instituted the complaint and I knew what motions I would file. I also knew I would arrange to take the borrower's deposition before asking him any written questions. I hoped to get the borrower to lie at his deposition and thus gain the opportunity to use his lie against him at trial.

A few days later I sent a memorandum to Hargrove outlining the strategy I would be following and explaining my reasoning. I also provided him with the hourly rates and billing policy that would apply to the case. Although I sent the memorandum by e-mail, nearly two weeks passed before Hargrove answered it. When his answer arrived, it made no reference to either the strategy or the billing matter. Hargrove simply stated that he had received my e-mail and understood what it said. He said he would be in touch with me if he had any questions. If it is possible for an e-mail message to reflect the writer's annoyance, Hargrove's did so.

As the case progressed, I provided Hargrove with customary status reports by e-mail. Sometimes he responded by acknowledging receipt of a message but never did he give me the slightest indication that he had read what I had sent. Once, when a matter arose that clearly required a decision on the part of the bank, I telephoned Hargrove to discuss the matter. What had originally sounded like annoyance quickly turned to disgust: "Look, this case is a fly speck to the bank, and I don't have time to read your e-mails or talk to you about things you should be able to decide without me." He made it clear that not only was the case insignificant to him, but that I was insignificant as well.

I ultimately negotiated a possible settlement of the case that I believed would be acceptable to the bank. This was relatively easy to accomplish since it was clear that the bank and the borrower would not be dealing with each other again. I wrote a letter to Hargrove advising him to accept the settlement and explaining my reasoning. Hargrove made the shortest possible response: "Settlement approved. Send final bill with settlement documents." There was no thank you, no reference to a good result, no closing remarks.

In thinking about what transpired with Hargrove, there are two possibilities: One is that his behavior had nothing to do with the case or me. The other is that Hargrove resented the need to have an outside lawyer do what he was unable to do. I would bet on the second possibility.

&a &a &a

# Dinner with Larry Flynt

A JOURNALIST FRIEND TELEPHONED one day to ask if I would represent *Hustler Magazine* in a case involving a constitutional matter. The case concerned whether military post exchanges could exclude *Hustler* while selling its two major competitors, *Playboy* and *Penthouse*. The military authorities would probably have preferred to exclude all three magazines, but they apparently considered *Hustler* to be more offensive than the others.

My friend arranged a dinner for the purpose of introducing me to Larry Flynt, the magazine's owner, so that he could determine whether he wanted to engage me. The dinner took place at a nice restaurant in the Georgetown section of Washington, D.C. Larry arrived unaccompanied. This surprised me because chief executives of corporations usually bring someone, perhaps an in-house lawyer, to such dinners. I came to the dinner with my wife, and my journalist friend brought one of his female employees.

I was aware, of course, that Larry had a reputation for being bluntly outspoken. He also had a reputation for pushing the envelope in a direction some considered pornography. The conversation at dinner flowed easily and it was clear fairly early in the meal that Larry had decided to use me.

The surprise at our dinner had nothing to do with the case, but, rather, concerned Larry's personality. He was anything but what his reputation suggested. My wife, who had no patience with vulgarity, commented afterwards that Larry was surprisingly soft-spoken and a perfect gentleman. Even when the conversation turned to sex, a topic to which Larry was no stranger, his choice of words and the tenor of his remarks could have survived a Sunday church meeting. It was interesting that a man of Larry's reputation behaved, at an informal dinner, in a way that belied it.

I undertook the representation of *Hustler Magazine* in the case, and it was ultimately settled in a satisfactory manner. I can't discuss privileged dealings with my client or its representatives, but I can say that every aspect of the engagement was in harmony with standard business practices.

❧ ❧ ❧

# Defending a Check Forger

I RECEIVED A PHONE call from a federal judge, asking if I would agree to defend an indigent woman accused of a crime. The payment for a court-appointed case is minimal, but I agreed and was advised that my new client was in the courthouse lockup. She would appear in court for the first time in approximately two hours. I had to get to the courthouse to meet her and discuss the case before she went to court.

At the courthouse I was greeted by a deputy marshal I had known for a long time. He told me my new client, Susan Pressley, was in the last cell at the back of the lockup, then took me there.

I was surprised by Susan's appearance. She had been arrested for cashing fraudulent checks in a number of states including Maryland. Her alleged actions violated federal laws, and she was arrested in Maryland by FBI agents. What surprised me was that Susan was nicely dressed and groomed and had the face of a college student. Most people I have seen arrested while on the run appear rather beat up and exhausted.

Susan told me her story in a forthright manner. There were difficulties in her family, including abandonment by Susan's mother. Susan was close to her mother and her absence was very painful for her. In her early twenties she had run away from home, settled in another state, and become an exotic dancer. She was more ashamed of that portion of her life than of the crimes that led to her arrest. Even after our short meeting, I liked Susan and felt she could do better in life.

The interesting thing that occurred as the case progressed was that I found my feeling about Susan was widely shared. The deputy marshal told me he felt that way about her. The federal agent who had arrested her felt that way about her. The probation officer who had prepared her presentence report felt that way about her. And, unlikely as it seems, the prosecutor felt that way about her. She had a veritable fan club in the courtroom.

When a plea bargain was reached, it was agreed that the prosecutor would make no specific recommendation at Susan's sentencing. I argued at sentencing for Susan to be placed on probation and not receive a jail sentence. I didn't expect the prosecutor to join in that recommendation but he did, and the probation officer who had prepared Susan's presentence report did so as well. The judge accepted the recommendation and Susan left the United States Courthouse when the hearing was finished.

Susan telephoned me a few weeks later to say she had reestablished her relationship with her family (excluding, of course, her mother who was never heard from again). She said she had found a good job and a nice place to live. Susan soon won the "Employee of the Year" award at her company.

A little less than a year later, Susan called to tell me she was engaged to be married. A year after that, she called to tell me she and her husband had just had their first baby. As I write this, I continue to receive calls from Susan every year during the holiday season.

ἔ ἔ ἔ

# Chronic Malpractice

A CLIENT OF MINE, a general surgeon, will give almost anything a try. My client is competent to perform appendectomies, gall bladder removals, and other routine operations, but he has no specialty training or experience. Nevertheless, if you put a scalpel in my client's hand and point him in the right direction, he's good to go. Fortunately for him, his malpractice insurance company is also good to go. My client has been sued for malpractice many times.

The first malpractice case I handled for him involved a procedure to remedy a misalignment in the patient's left foot. This condition results in great difficulty in walking. The condition is one that definitely requires surgery.

The remedy for this condition is a complicated operation that requires specialty, if not subspecialty, training and experience. When I looked in anatomy books to prepare myself for the case, I saw more parts than imaginable in a person's foot. There were bones, nerves, tendons, blood vessels, and other, more mysterious parts, intricately connected to form the complex structure that supports the entire body. It didn't take a rocket scientist to conclude that a general surgeon attempting to do this operation is about as qualified for it as a glider pilot is to fly a 747. Fortunately, a competent orthopaedic surgeon was able to remedy the damage my client had done and the case was settled for an amount within the limit of his insurance policy. I was naive enough to believe he had learned his lesson.

The next time my client decided to perform an operation about which he knew nothing the consequences were more serious. The operation involved a problem in the testicles of a man in his thirties. The procedure is difficult and delicate and misperformance of it has serious consequences. The procedure must be performed by a surgeon with specialty training.

My client botched this operation and his patient wasn't a happy camper. The patient sued for an amount well in excess of my client's insurance coverage and engaged a capable lawyer to represent him. The case was difficult to settle within the coverage limit of my client's malpractice insurance policy.

After the case ended, one of my partners and I often joked about this client. Our jokes involved suggesting that he give brain surgery a try. It was clear by this time that his judgment about what surgery he should perform was sorely defective.

Fortunately, the hospital where my client performed surgery recognized that his choices were reckless and implemented a second-opinion requirement to avoid future difficulties. My client was able to competently perform operations for which he was qualified.

ða ða ða

# A Suicidal Client

AN ACCOUNTANT WHO WAS my client faced loss of his license because he had falsified critical documents. In spite of his dishonesty, I liked this accountant. On an occasion early in the case, as we sat in my conference room discussing what he had done, he told me how his mother, who had cheered him through accounting school and the CPA exams, would feel if he were to lose his license.

A balcony with a waist-high rail is outside the conference room we were using. A door at the rear of the room opens onto the balcony. During our conversation, I saw my client looking forlornly at the door. He suggested he might as well jump off the balcony (falling twenty-six stories to the pavement). His remark was the sort of thing people say when they believe their plight is hopeless and I didn't take it seriously until he repeated it two times. At that point I told him that he was making me nervous and I felt ill-equipped to deal with his emotional state. I asked him whether he would let me telephone a psychiatrist I know and tell him what was going on. My client agreed and I made the call. The psychiatrist made an appointment with my client for the next day.

I spoke with the psychiatrist after the appointment to inquire about my client. He told me my client was close enough to suicide to require immediate psychiatric care. He had started him on medication and had scheduled a series of appointments with him.

The next time he came to my office my client brought his mother with him. The charges against my client had been resolved favorably and his mental state was vastly improved. His mother, who knew nothing about the falsified documents, thought her son had been treated unfairly. "He's a fine boy," she told me, "they were much too hard on him."

# Others

## Preface

IN ADDITION TO CLIENTS, lawyers deal regularly with many others. These include participants in transactions and businesses, witnesses in cases, experts, judges and administrators, other lawyers, all sorts of functionaries, spouses and significant others, families and friends, public officials and employees. It is fair to say that lawyers deal with people about as often as traveling salesmen.

Some of the most interesting and memorable incidents that occur in the practice of law involve people who are not clients. Since there is no attorney-client privilege between lawyers and people who are not clients, such incidents generally arise in unpredictable circumstances and not as a result of communications with the other person. Lawyers have no professional obligations to people who are not their clients, other than to be courteous, truthful and respectful. Some such incidents would, in fact, never arise if the other person was a client.

Dealings with other people affect the outcome of clients' cases in many ways. A good witness or a convincing expert can determine the outcome of a trial. Another party in a particular matter or the lawyer representing that party can radically change the course of events from a client's point of view. A difficult public official can make something otherwise possible to accomplish inconceivable. No lawyer could properly serve a client without taking into account the personalities of other people affecting that client.

The essays that follow deal with people other than clients who have affected the outcome of a client's case and, in some instances, profoundly affected me. Such people include an individual who was shot and paralyzed by an assailant, a witness who had convinced himself of a fabricated part of his history and a nurse who conducted a seamless triage of the victims of a terrible bus accident. Some of the most dramatic incidents I recall took place with people other than clients.

ટ ટ ટ

# Meeting with George Wallace

I MET GOVERNOR GEORGE Wallace of Alabama under unusual circumstances. He was campaigning for the office of President of the United States when he was shot by a strange young man named Arthur Bremer during a campaign rally at a shopping center in Maryland. Bremer was immediately taken to Baltimore by the Secret Service where he was charged with a federal crime. Shortly thereafter, he was also charged with a state crime.

I turned out to be the federal prosecutor in charge of the Bremer case. It was certainly not a case requiring special skill. The shooting had been recorded by television cameras and observed by many witnesses, including Secret Service agents. Although I prepared the case carefully for the grand jury, it was impossible for any problem to arise. Bremer was indicted by the grand jury about a week after the shooting.

Insofar as the case against Arthur Bremer was concerned, there was no need for me to see Governor Wallace. I decided, however, to visit him in his room at Holy Cross Hospital in Silver Spring, Maryland, as a professional courtesy and to assure him that federal prosecution of Bremer was proceeding. Governor Wallace probably knew everything there was to know about the Bremer case from extensive media coverage.

George Wallace was not a blank slate for me when I visited him in his hospital room with two colleagues. For most Americans of my generation, Wallace was the embodiment of segregation. His face, particularly his jutting jaw and perpetual grimace, was an iconic mask of racial prejudice to virtually everyone. Wallace stood in schoolhouse doors to prevent black children from entering and he stated publicly his desire to see apartheid continue forever in this country. I had this image of George Wallace in my mind as my two colleagues and I went through the line of Secret Service agents cordoning off one-half of the top floor of Holy Cross Hospital.

As we entered the room, I was immediately aware that Wallace was in great distress. A bar running the length of his bed supported his body and I knew from public sources that the bullet had paralyzed him. Even with Wallace's infamous history in mind, the sight we saw aroused sympathy for a man grievously injured and suffering greatly.

Wallace did not offer us a seat and I placed my attaché case next to me on the floor. From our positions he assumed correctly that I would be doing the talking. My remarks were simple and straightforward: He had been shot by a man named Arthur Bremer about whom very little was known. Bremer had been arrested, taken to Baltimore for an initial appearance before the federal court, and incarcerated. I told Governor Wallace I would take the case to a federal grand jury as promptly as possible and I was sure I possessed sufficient evidence to secure an indictment. Wallace had no comments or questions about these remarks but instead went directly to another subject.

The newspapers and broadcast media referred to a "diary" that was found in Bremer's car. The diary outlined Bremer's wanderings since leaving his job as a busboy in Milwaukee. It indicated that Bremer had followed and identified as targets numerous individuals during his travels. It was clear from the diary that Governor Wallace had not been shot by Bremer for any particular reason.

Governor Wallace was intensely interested in knowing about the diary and he asked me directly, "You got a copy of it?" I told him that I had a copy in my attaché case and he asked me if he could see it. When I handed it to him he immediately began reading it. My colleagues and I stood there in silence for several minutes until he asked me if he could keep the diary to read it entirely. I told him he could and he should return it to one of the Secret Service agents when he was finished.

There wasn't much more to my visit with Governor Wallace. At no time were remarks of a personal nature made by any of us. I had met a man considered to be the most infamous bigot in public life. I had also met a man who would suffer so intensely that he would some day go to a black church and repent before its congregation for what he had done to black people. Wallace would explain there that he had learned from the shooting how much suffering a person can experience. I did not see Wallace's repentance, but years later I saw the actor Gary Sinise play Wallace in a reenactment of it. I believe I saw Wallace in his hospital room at the genesis of his repentance.

Notwithstanding its brevity, my experience with Governor Wallace affected me more than I would have imagined. It isn't possible for one to feel stronger dislike for an individual than I felt for Governor Wallace at the time I met him, but it's possible to feel sympathy for the same person.

❧ ❧ ❧

# An Illegal Immigrant

*CON CUIDADO!* I'M SHOUTING from my seat on the porch to a work-man in the yard who has climbed a tree and is leaning over with a chain-saw to remove a dead limb. The small man with neatly cropped jet-black hair and a forlorn expression has been working tirelessly for several hours since the landscape company dropped him off. I don't know this man, but I know enough to conjure his story: He's from Mexico or Central Amer-ica and has undertaken great risks to come to the United States. He has relatives back home, perhaps a wife and children, who rely on his earn-ings. He frequents the store a half mile from my house that transfers money for Spanish-speaking customers to places south of the border. He lives in squalid conditions in a house crowded with other such men like the circus cars when we were kids.

The State of Arizona has passed a law known as the "Support Our Law Enforcement and Safe Neighborhoods Act." The Arizona law is intended to increase the ability of police officers to arrest illegal immi-grants so that they may be removed from our country. Supporters of the Arizona law envision such people as evil aliens who violate our borders and flaunt our laws.

The federal government has sued the State of Arizona to enjoin enforcement of the Arizona law. It contends the field of immigration is preempted by federal law. Other states are carefully watching what is occurring in Arizona. Some are considering similar laws.

The workman is now coming down from the tree and placing the severed limb in a pile he has assembled. He is breathing heavily and drenched in perspiration. His sleeveless T-shirt and oversize shorts hang limply from his body. He barely stops working long enough to catch his breath.

I go to the kitchen and take a Coke from the refrigerator and cross the yard and offer it to the workman. *Quieres un Coke?* He looks at me sideways and fearfully, wondering if I'm thinking about his immigration status. *No necessita,* he tells me, but his parched lips and dripping chin tell me otherwise. *De nada,* I tell him and push the Coke into his hand.

Federal Judge Susan Bolton has ruled on the government's motion for a preliminary injunction. She has carefully examined each provision of the law and determined that the federal government is likely to suc-ceed at trial with respect to four provisions. She has determined that irreparable harm would be suffered if she did not enjoin enforcement of those provisions. Judge Bolton's judicial craftsmanship was excellent. From a lawyer's viewpoint, she did her work perfectly.

The landscape company's truck is arriving in front of the house and the workman takes the pile of limbs and branches and places it on the truck. There are two other men in the back of the truck, by their look also Hispanic. The truck drives off with the three men in the back. I will probably never again see the workman I have been watching.

I will think about a small man with neatly cropped jet-black hair and a forlorn expression every time I hear about the matter of illegal immigrants. I will hope there is room within the laws of our country to notice that he is a good worker, that he is lonely and far from home and that he gets thirsty on hot summer days.

## On the Red Eye

I'M TAKING A RED-eye flight from San Jose, California, to Baltimore-Washington International. I have worked in San Jose for several days and every night I spend in a hotel is one night too many. I'm familiar with red-eye flights from California. I sleep better on the plane than in any hotel room.

The seats, spacing and service are far better in the business section of airplanes, but there is one problem. The problem is that you have only one chance of getting a satisfactory seatmate. The slightly angry, officious-looking lady with a tightly compressed bun at the back of her head coming down the aisle will undoubtedly spoil that chance for me. When she stops next to my seat and checks her boarding pass, I know that my desire to sleep undisturbed until we reach the East Coast will not be satisfied. Since I have the aisle seat, she squirms her way with a slightly disgusted gasp to the window.

Even before we take off, my seatmate has given me a good part of her life story. She's a librarian from a suburb of Washington, has never married, and is returning from visiting her sister, a clerk of some kind in Palo Alto. I infer that both the sisters are spinsters. From the way my seatmate describes her work, I'm definitely in the company of someone who has totally mastered the Dewey Decimal System.

When it's my turn to reveal my credentials, my seatmate turns to me and, in a slightly hostile tone, asks, "So, what do you do?" I'm inclined to tell her that I'm an artificial insemination donor and don't wish to discuss the particulars of my work. My sense of decorum holds me back, however. I'm trying to think of an answer that will forestall the interrogation I know is forthcoming, but my mind is not quick enough.

"I'm a lawyer."

"What kind of cases do you handle?"

"I do a lot of different things."

I can see that she's ready for the main event and can think of no way to stop her: "Do you defend any criminals?"

"Sometimes."

"I don't understand how you can defend people you know are guilty."

She has laid down the moral gauntlet and, to make her separation from the odious heathen beside her absolutely clear, she moves to the far side of her seat. My choice is simple: I can explain to her why her question is idiotic, why she has no understanding whatsoever of the constitutional right to a defense attorney, why she would never want to live in a country where a committee of librarians decided who was worthy of a defense, and why it's more difficult to defend a person you know is innocent than one you know is guilty. I know nothing would be accomplished by providing such explanations, and I choose the other option. The other option is to tell my righteous seatmate I must get some sleep so I can continue my misguided work in the morning.

As I close my eyes and try to begin my badly needed four or five hour sleep, I see my seatmate placing an object against her side of the armrest between us. I assume the armrest has now become a moral interface. On one side (hers) every form of morality is manifest. On the other side (mine) there exists unmitigated depravity in the form of a person who aligns himself with the most degenerate members of society. I'm grateful to be falling asleep.

ໃ▲ ໃ▲ ໃ▲

# Law School Job

MY FIRST LEGAL JOB was as a "lien unit clerk" in the Tax Division of the Justice Department. The function of the three law students who had this job was simple: we were to determine whether complaints that were filed against the United States contained six specific elements required by the law. If a complaint did, the United States became a party to the case. If it did not, the lawyer for the United States filed a motion to dismiss, which would be granted. The matter was important to people who wanted to establish the priority of their liens. Complaints came from all fifty states.

A few weeks into the job I began to notice certain trends among the complaints. I noticed that complaints from certain states, particularly those in the Southwest, were invariably flawless. I also noticed that complaints from certain other states, particularly New York, frequently paid no attention to what the law required. After a month or two I went to the woman who had supervised lien unit clerks for many years and told her of my observation. Her response was direct and immediate: "You've noticed what almost every lien unit clerk notices sooner or later. There are wide regional differences in the care lawyers take to comply with the law. Don't hold your breath waiting for a complaint from Oklahoma that isn't perfect."

Years later this experience came back to me when I had a client who made machinery in Albuquerque, New Mexico. I became friendly with several New Mexico lawyers who worked with me, in particular one named Barclay Cranston. Barclay didn't know how to write a letter or a legal document that wasn't perfect. He was a soft-spoken, guileless man, and I came to trust and rely on him as the best sort of colleague.

There came a time when my client changed its banking relationship from a large New York bank to a midsize bank that had branches in Southwestern states, including New Mexico. A large well-known New York law firm represented the New York bank that my client was leaving. A very experienced and pleasant lawyer in Dallas represented the Southwestern bank that was establishing a relationship with my client. Barclay and I represented the machine manufacturer.

Very soon after the dealings between lawyers had begun, their stylistic differences became obvious. The New York lawyers behaved pompously, although their legal work was sloppy. Barclay and the Texas lawyer behaved in the straightforward, courteous way typical of southwestern lawyers. Their written materials were perfect and they never mentioned the deficiencies in the materials presented by the New York lawyers.

As the lawyers for the outgoing and incoming banks got into the most difficult aspects of the work, the rudeness of the New York lawyers became extraordinary. One of them would say to Barclay or the Texas lawyer something like, "I don't know if you've ever been involved in a refinancing before, but in our shop we deal with these things every day, and we know what we're doing." On one occasion one of the New York lawyers said, "I don't know what kind of legal work you guys do down there, but up here we work on refinancings large enough to buy New Mexico." For the most part, I escaped such treatment, probably because the New York lawyers knew I also was born in New York City and now worked there from time to time.

Since I was the only lawyer in a position to do so, I tried more than once to get the New York lawyers to back off from their insults. Barclay knew I was doing my best, but it was clear I was failing. Barclay's kind remarks to me while the insults flew let me know that notwithstanding my being raised in New York, I was not considered a New York lawyer like those with whom we were dealing.

Barclay's final comment about the New York lawyers after the refinancing was concluded was: "I will not soon forget the way they acted." I will not soon forget the way the New York lawyers acted and the way Barclay and the lawyer from Texas responded. I'd like to think I could in similar circumstances exercise as much restraint.

ॐ ॐ ॐ

# Misconduct by Adverse Party

I REPRESENTED A BIRTH control clinic in a zoning matter. Although instigated by a right-to-life constituency, the case had nothing to do with the
highly charged issue between proponents of the right to life and of freedom of choice. I provided exactly the same services to my client as I
would have provided had I represented a client who advanced the interests of right-to-life proponents.

Two disquieting things happened while the zoning hearing was taking place: The first was my pregnant wife's receipt of an anonymous letter telling her that if people like her husband had their way, she wouldn't
be delivering a live baby. The second was that some of the people who
had instigated the zoning matter brought very young children to the
hearing room and seated them in the front row.

I told the lawyer representing the other side of the zoning matter
about the letter my wife had received. I also told him that I thought it
was inappropriate to bring young children to a legal hearing where they
obviously had no function. With regard to both matters I told my colleague that his clients should not assume anything about my personal
views regarding the controversial issue, reminding him that the legal matter we were addressing concerned zoning and nothing else.

I don't know what action, if any, my colleague took in response to
what I told him. There was no further action taken with regard to the letter my wife received, and after being present for a full day, the children
never reappeared in the hearing room. The hearing judge concluded that
my client was not in violation of the zoning laws.

&a &a &a

# Dinner with Mr. and Mrs. Shriver

I NEVER IMAGINED I would have a private dinner with Sargent Shriver and his wife, Eunice Kennedy Shriver, and one of their children. People who run for Vice President of the United States and members of the Kennedy family are way out of my league.

I met Sargent Shriver in the course of advising one of his sons with regard to a business matter. Mr. Shriver would telephone me from time to time to receive an update on the progress of the matter and make suggestions. From the outset it was obvious to me that Mr. Shriver was a concerned parent. After the matter was completed, I spoke with Mr. Shriver once or twice when he had questions concerning legal matters in Baltimore. On one of those occasions he asked me if I would provide legal services to another of his sons who was running an exceptional program for troubled young men in Baltimore. Needless to say, I was eager to do so.

Shortly thereafter, I met with Mark Shriver, the son conducting the program, for breakfast. Mark has features of his uncle, Robert Kennedy. It was difficult to avoid remembering the overwhelming sadness I felt the morning I learned of Robert Kennedy's death. I believed then, and I believe now, that Robert Kennedy as President would have changed the course of this country.

The dinner came about very simply. Mark telephoned me one afternoon and told me that his parents were coming to Baltimore for dinner and they wanted to know if I would join them. My answer to Mark's question was a no-brainer. I telephoned my wife and told her of my unlikely dinner plans.

Mr. and Mrs. Shriver, Mark and I met for dinner at a private club located on a high floor of an office building directly overlooking Baltimore's Inner Harbor. Although I made the reservation, I hadn't known how many people would be joining us. I anticipated other guests but the Shrivers arrived accompanied only by Mark. We were seated at a window table directly overlooking the harbor. Mr. and Mrs. Shriver were on one side of the table, Mark and I on the other.

From the moment of Mark's invitation, I felt certain there was some special agenda involving me to be discussed. At each juncture of the dinner, after we finished our appetizers, after we finished the main course, after we finished dessert, and when coffee finally arrived, I felt certain the real purpose of the dinner would be revealed. It never was.

I couldn't help noticing as we ate that the Shrivers shared an intimacy that was probably obvious to anyone. At times Mr. Shriver would take hold of his wife's hand above the table. At other times they seemed almost lost in shared recollections. I particularly recall a remark Mrs. Shriver made to her husband. A large yacht, so large it had to moor at the end of one of the piers rather than in a boat slip, arrived at the Inner Harbor Marina while we were eating. The yacht was ablaze with lights and all of us turned to look at it. Mrs. Shriver leaned over towards her husband, who was sitting closer to the window, and recalled the time President Kennedy had invited them aboard the Presidential Yacht somewhere off Cape Cod.

Mrs. Shriver's remark had nothing to do with John Kennedy's Presidency nor anything concerning the celebrity of the Kennedy family. It was irrelevant that Mrs. Shriver's brother had been a President of the United States, that the sight that aroused her recollection was a glorious yacht, or that her husband to whom she made the remark had run for the office of Vice President. The remark was that of a sister whose brother had been killed and whom she greatly missed.

Perhaps it was this incident that finally, as we finished our coffee, awakened me to the understanding that this dinner had no undisclosed agenda. The Shrivers were simply parents saying thank you for the help I had given their son. It was a misassumption on my part that such people don't operate without an agenda and express themselves like all loving parents. I felt embarrassed as this realization came to me. I will probably not have another such dinner in my life, but if I do it won't take until the last sips of coffee for me to realize that there are no special families insofar as parents and their children are concerned.★

---

★After my dinner with the Shrivers and their son, my wife and I had the privilege of being invited to their home for their son's engagement party. In the public part of the Shrivers' house hang framed letters from John and Robert Kennedy to members of their family, letters written before they occupied public offices. A friend and I were reading the letters when Mrs. Shriver came over and graciously explained some things about them. The next morning my friend telephoned to tell me about a dream he had that John and Robert Kennedy's sister was talking to him about letters her brothers had written. I told my friend that was an amazing coincidence because I had the same dream.

ZA ZA ZA

# Nurse's Triage

FOR SEVERAL YEARS MY busiest client was a hospital in a bedroom community about 20 miles north of Baltimore. I visited the hospital frequently to attend meetings and discuss matters with department heads and administrators. I have always been interested in medicine and my work for the hospital provided many opportunities to see it practiced.

There were exciting situations over the years. On two occasions I obtained court orders permitting blood transfusions for children of Jehovah's Witness families. On one occasion I approved the release of a patient A.M.A. (against medical advice) when the patient chose to die of internal bleeding rather than receive medical care. There were all sorts of malpractice cases, ranging from situations where there was clearly no medical negligence to a few cases where medical negligence was indisputable. On numerous occasions I provided legal advice affecting people's lives. There was no shortage of drama in my work for the hospital.

A particular situation is lodged firmly in my memory. It was a situation in which I had no function.

I parked at the hospital in a staff parking lot behind the main building. The door I used to enter the hospital was also used by ambulances bringing patients to the emergency room. The emergency room directly adjoined the corridor leading to the rest of the hospital.

Usually when I arrived at the hospital one or two ambulances blocked the door, but on this occasion I found at least a dozen ambulances with flashers going and numerous police cars as well. People with obviously serious injuries were being taken on gantries and stretchers to the emergency room. The scene was warlike and I had to wait several minutes for the doorway to clear before I could enter the hospital. One of the police officers told me that a fully loaded bus had rolled over on the nearby interstate highway.

I would have passed the emergency room and headed straight to my meeting, but something I saw out of the corner of my eye stopped me. What I saw was a nurse whom I recognized standing just inside the emergency room door conducting a triage. The nurse briefly examined each patient and received whatever information the accompanying attendants were able to provide her.

The memorable thing about the nurse conducting the triage was her calmness and grace. Patients were arriving with injuries from minor contusions to life-threatening injuries. Some patients had only external injuries and others suffered from internal bleeding and injuries to vital organs. The triage nurse made her determinations quickly and gave directions to other nurses as to each patient.

"Stella, please intubate this gentlemen and give him two cc's of Ativan. He will require surgery as soon as possible."

"Myra, this lady has quite a bit of bleeding. Please begin her drip immediately and order a type and cross stet."

"Judy, this gentleman can walk and has only superficial contusions. Please clean him up quickly and seat him over there."

My stepfather was chief of surgery of a front-line hospital during World War II. He told me many times that he often performed the triage himself. I was thinking of him as I watched the nurse performing the same function. When my stepfather told me about the triage, I realized that one who conducts it is making rapid life-and-death decisions with no opportunity for reconsideration. The triage nurse I was watching was doing precisely that. If the man just seated to await treatment for superficial contusions had, in fact, a serious internal injury, the triage nurse's decision might cost him his life. What amazed me was that she performed the triage seamlessly and unemotionally. It was like seeing a ballerina perform a routine she has practiced a thousand times.

I watched the triage nurse for at least 15 minutes. I watched her so long that I was late for the meeting I had come to the hospital to attend. As I sat down and joined the discussion dealing with a new program for otolaryngology residents, I felt that the meeting was taking place in slow motion. The participants had plenty of time to consider what they were saying, to qualify or retract it, and even to reverse a determination if they wished.

## Transfusion

AT ABOUT 5 O'CLOCK one morning I received a call from Dr. Charles Hammond, chief of emergency medical services at a county hospital I had represented for about four years. I knew Dr. Hammond from my involvement in the negotiation of his group's contract to provide emergency services to the hospital. Charles was a generally well-controlled man who usually began conversations with a few pleasantries. On this occasion his tone was urgent and it was clear he would skip his customary greeting:

> I have a very serious case here. It's a nine-year-old boy with a deep contusion in his left leg. He's lost a lot of blood, probably two units, and needs a transfusion immediately. The boy was brought to the hospital by his mother, who refused to permit him to receive a blood transfusion. I've told her that irreparable injury to her son is almost certain and death is possible if he is not transfused. She won't budge and I'm out of options. We have compatible blood at the bedside and I need you to get a court order immediately.

This was the second such case I have had. In the first case the patient, a fourteen-year-old girl, had suffered an abdominal wound in a fall and had lost a lot of blood before she and her parents arrived at the hospital. Her parents were both Jehovah's Witnesses and adamantly opposed to blood transfusion. Obtaining a court order was not difficult and, as soon as the parents were advised of it, they refrained from further interference. Their daughter was transfused and recovered very well.

"Do you know where the father is?" I asked Charles. "No, I don't, but the mother said he was unavailable. We don't have time to look for him. The boy's hematocrit is well below the red-line and he's white and breathing very deeply. Without blood, I think he won't live."

Every county in Maryland has an emergency judge available at all times for situations such as this one, and I had both the judges' schedule for the hospital's county and, luckily, their home numbers. I put Charles on hold while I called the judge. It was immediately obvious that I had awakened Judge Herman Waxter. When I introduced myself, the judge remembered me from appearances in his court and knew I was the hospital's general counsel and would not call at this hour if it were not an emergency. I had Charles join the call so he and I could explain the situation without delay. I spoke quickly:

Judge, there is a nine-year-old boy in the emergency room being attended by Dr. Charles Hammond, chief of emergency medical services. The boy has a deep contusion in his leg and has lost a great deal of blood. He's showing signs of serious impending injury and possibly death. Dr. Hammond has the necessary blood available at the boy's bedside but his mother is a Jehovah's Witness and refuses to consent to a transfusion. She is the only person accompanying the boy. I am asking for an emergency oral order providing three things: one, that the medical care of the boy be turned over to Dr. Hammond; two, that all persons be enjoined from interfering with Dr. Hammond; and, three, that I be authorized as an officer of the court to announce the order to all persons present and to seek the assistance of law enforcement officers, if necessary, to enforce it. I will provide you with a written order.

Judge Waxter asked only one question: "Dr. Hammond, are you certain that in the absence of a blood transfusion serious irreparable injury and possibly death will result?" Charles's reply was instant: "I couldn't be more certain, Judge. There isn't any physician who would consider not transfusing this boy."

I got into my car and left for the hospital, telling Charles to get started while I was on my way. I rehearsed two speeches as I drove. One was what I would tell the police officer who would undoubtedly stop me for speeding. The other was what I would tell the people at the hospital, including the child's mother. As it turned out, my rehearsals proved unnecessary. I was not stopped for speeding, and when I arrived the boy's mother was sitting quietly on a bench in the hallway outside the emergency room. When I entered the emergency room I saw a bag of blood hanging from a pole and blood was already running through a tube into the boy's arm.

After all the excitement, there was nothing for me to do. I spoke briefly with Charles, who was enormously relieved. Then I left the emergency room and sat down with the boy's mother. She did not appear to be upset. There was no need to advise her about what the court had ordered, since Charles had already done that. Obviously, it was not appropriate to discuss religious convictions with her, and I didn't. What I told her was that it was likely that her son would recover fully from his injury and that he was receiving the best possible medical care from Dr. Hammond.

As was true in the other case involving Jehovah's Witnesses, I had the distinct impression that the boy's mother was pleased that her authority had been curtailed by the court. I couldn't read her mind, but I believe she had expected what had occurred. The boy recovered fully and nothing was heard from his mother or from anyone else.

≈ ≈ ≈

# A Cultural Mistake

ANOTHER LAWYER AND I went to Thailand to interview government witnesses in a Foreign Corrupt Practices Act investigation. Our client was an American tank manufacturer. The Foreign Corrupt Practices Act prohibits American corporations from using agents in foreign countries who make unlawful payments to facilitate sales. In this case, the sales were to the Thai military and the agents had allegedly paid government officials to facilitate them. Truth be told, it's impossible to sell anything larger than an egg in Southeast Asia without an official being paid off.

Before we arrived in Bangkok, we engaged the services of a Thai lawyer who was fluent in English and familiar with American and Thai legal systems. The agents were ambivalent about speaking with us. They valued their business with our client, which was very lucrative, but they feared the consequences of an investigation that might implicate them in unlawful conduct. The agents agreed to speak with us in an office in Bangkok, but they were not enthusiastic. The agents' responses to our inquiries were constrained from the outset and their expressions remained implacable throughout our visit. I told the first agent that I was going to do the questioning and he responded with indifference.

My colleague was a woman and the first indication of a cultural gap came about as a result of the matter of sex. She was the repository of all relevant facts. I turned to my colleague regularly when questions of fact arose. The agents quickly realized that she was the factual authority, but Thai custom precluded their speaking directly to her. Instead, the agents would look at me, speaking in a fashion that made it clear that my colleague heard them, and then wait for her to provide me with information. I became annoyed with being a sort of mock translator, but there was nothing I could do about it. Women are not recognized as having professional status in Thailand.

A more difficult problem arising out of cultural incongruities occurred when I questioned the first agent about his knowledge of a particular individual. The question concerned the agent's relationship with government officials. I asked the agent whether he knew a general named Sudamalanga. The answer I received was, "I don't know him." Since I knew the agent knew General Sudamalanga and that he had visited him and had dinner with him one evening, I knew his answer to be untrue by American standards.

I persisted for a while in variations on my question. Each time the answer was the same: "I don't know him." I then referred the agent to the meeting at General Sudamalanga's office: "Didn't you go to General Sudamalanga's office on February 23 of last year to see him about specific details of the tanks, such as speed and weight?" Instead of answering my question, the agent repeated his line: "I don't know him." I referred the agent to the dinner I knew he had with General Sudamalanga, even naming the restaurant where it took place. His answer was the same and my frustration was becoming obvious.

At that point, the Thai lawyer we had engaged asked me and my colleague if we could take a short break and go out into the hallway. We agreed and walked out of the room and went to the far end of the hallway. There my colleague and I received a lesson in Thai culture.

In Thailand, the matter of knowledge of another person is not a unified concept as in the United States. If one is asked in the United States, "do you know Mr. X?" the answer is "yes" if you know Mr. X in any context whatsoever. In Thailand, however, one knows people in one context but not in another. Our Thai colleague explained that this custom grew out of the exigencies of living in communal dwellings with other families. Many Thais live in such fashion and for particular purposes they do not "know" the members of the other families. Our Thai colleague provided us with a Thai word for the custom.

In the case of the agent I was questioning, what was occurring was that the agent didn't know what sort of knowledge I was referring to and therefore took the safe course of disclaiming any knowledge of General Sudamalanga. To receive the answer we needed, I would have to revise my question to make it clear that I was asking the agent whether he knew General Sudamalanga in a particular context. My Thai colleague gave me the exact wording to use and we returned to the room where we were working. When I asked the question the way my Thai colleague had worded it for me, I immediately received an affirmative answer explaining that the agent knew General Sudamalanga in the context I had described.

I attribute my ultimate success to two things: First, I had been instructed by my Thai colleague as to how to ask the question the right way. Second, the agent obviously saw my Thai colleague take the silly Americans into the hall and explain to them why I was getting nowhere.

ᘒ ᘒ ᘒ

# Proving Parentage

I ONCE HAD A case involving what is known as "bastardy." The purpose of such a case is to establish the parentage of a child born out of wedlock. In this case, the mother had custody of the child and the father had always acknowledged his fatherhood.

The father of the child, a girl, had often given her birthday and holiday gifts. He spent time with her regularly. Religious documents designated him as the father. Everyone who knew the situation believed the father had acknowledged his parentage. Nevertheless, for reasons I never understood, the father was unwilling to have it legally established that the girl was his daughter.

I filed a lawsuit on my client's behalf, but the case never came to trial. When I took the father's deposition and placed on the record the many confirmations of his having acknowledged fathering the girl, it was certain we would win the case. Shortly after the deposition, the father's lawyer contacted me to say his client was willing to make legal acknowledgment of his parental status. I never understood why legal proceedings were necessary for him to do so.

Years later, I was sitting in a coffee shop having breakfast on my way to work. The mother who had engaged me entered, followed by an attractive teenage girl. "Hi, it's good to see you. I'd like to introduce you to your client." Smiling broadly, she moved aside so I could get a full view of her daughter. It pleased me to know that both her parents were legally confirmed. It isn't often that a lawyer receives gratification for work a decade and a half after it has been done.

### A Special Defense

THE PROSECUTION'S CASE AGAINST Morris Hernbach couldn't have been stronger. Morris was charged with overbilling a government agency for expenses. The proof of the overbilling was airtight. I had expense vouchers in Morris's name for each of the billings. Although Morris had hired the best attorney for such a case that money could buy, even Steve Sachs couldn't get a not-guilty verdict for him if there were to be a trial.

Lawyers have a saying: "When the law is against you, argue the facts; when the facts are against you, argue the law; when both are against you, pray." I don't know whether Steve prayed for Morris, but the solution he pursued worked like a charm. Steve out-lawyered me in Morris's case.

Steve's approach began by discussing facts with me that only Morris could establish. Although Steve's contentions were a bit far-fetched, they were plausible enough to interest me. He argued that if I knew the facts of the case, I would recommend that Morris be placed on probation.

Steve then suggested a possibility that defense attorneys occasionally raise with prosecutors. He suggested bringing Morris to my office to discuss the case and answer questions. The understanding was that nothing Morris said would be used against him if there were a trial. I agreed to permit Steve to bring Morris to my office.

Steve brought Morris to my office on a day that was stifling hot. As usual, the air-conditioning in the federal courthouse was sorely deficient. The three of us sat in my office perspiring profusely while Morris explained various matters about his overbillings. His explanations were not very persuasive, and I didn't understand until later that they were not Steve's purpose in bringing Morris to see me.

At a certain point in the meeting Steve got up quickly, said that the heat was unbearable, and he was going to get us some Cokes. He walked out of my office before either Morris or I could respond. Although places that sold Cokes were steps away from the courthouse, Steve must have decided the Coke was better on the other side of town. It took him at least forty-five minutes to acquire three Cokes in plastic containers with barely any ice remaining.

Morris and I sat in silence for a minute or two after Steve left. Because it would have been improper to discuss the case without Steve present, I broke the silence by asking Morris where he came from. As it turned out, Morris came from the same part of New York City where I grew up. Moreover, he too was the son of a Russian immigrant, had attended the same sort of school I had, engaged in the same activities as I had, and had frequented the same places I had. By the time Steve returned it had occurred to me that Morris and I might be related. Since Steve knew my background was identical with Morris's, this was hardly a coincidence. When Steve returned, Morris and I were having a lively conversation punctuated by laughter.

The purpose of Steve's plan was to make it emotionally impossible for me to recommend that Morris be incarcerated. His plan succeeded. It would be like putting myself in jail. Steve and I agreed on a plea bargain whereby Morris would admit to one of the offenses with which he was charged and I would recommend probation. Morris Hernbach never spent a day in jail. I never waited longer for a Coke.

ﾞ🐾 ﾞ🐾 ﾞ🐾

# Death of a Jockey

I RECEIVED A PHONE call from a lawyer in Arizona, who asked me if I would represent the family of a jockey who had been killed in a racing accident at Pimlico Racetrack. The jockey had been crushed when his horse slipped and fell over another horse that had broken down. The horse that broke down had been given an illegal drug, and our job was to prove that the drug caused the horse to collapse.

The jockey's family consisted of his wife, three young children and his parents who lived in a community where Spanish was the primary language spoken. I met the widow and her children soon after the accident and had no difficulty agreeing with the widow on how the case would be handled. The parents of the jockey, however, were another story. They refused to come to Baltimore or even go to the office of the Arizona lawyer who referred the case to me.

We agreed to visit the deceased jockey's parents in their home. Since my ability to speak Spanish is quite limited, my colleague who referred the case, and who was fluent in Spanish, agreed to join me. Even with the translation matter out of the way, the parents were reluctant to speak about the case. In the course of our meeting I learned that their other son had also been killed in a work-related accident. The uncanny loss of both sons in accidents had numbed the parents beyond words.

When the case was concluded, at least three years later, I agreed with the widow to allocate a small portion of the money received to the parents. I sent the parents copies of legal documents confirming what we were doing and enclosed a check payable to them. I received confirmation that my letter arrived at the parents' house. About a week later, with no explanation, the jockey's parents returned the check I had sent them. I never heard anything further from them, and ultimately gave the money to the widow.

ð ð ð

# Death of a Lawyer

I WAS JUST ADVISED that a lawyer I have liked and admired for many years has died. The lawyer was of the generation before mine. I got to know him in several ways, particularly when working for a client who had purchased a large parcel of land from a client of his to build an office building. On one occasion I had lunch with this lawyer and always wondered whether he knew how privileged I felt to have a private conversation with him.

The deceased lawyer reminded me of the stepfather who raised me from my teenage years to manhood and the practice of law. My stepfather was a surgeon and his interests and experience ranged widely. Men like them are like a good stew on its second day: the ingredients, each superior in its own right, blend subtly to become a masterpiece. In my experience, such men are always part of what Tom Brokaw called "the greatest generation." A central ingredient of this formidable stew was coming of age during the years this country was engaged in World War II. It's possible for a person of my generation to know facts and figures about World War II, as the generation that lived through it did. It's impossible, however, for anyone of my generation to know the tenor of a time when all Americans felt proud of what our country was doing.

The deceased lawyer's generation was the last to understand that a great lawyer is more than one who has mastered the law. A great lawyer is a generalist, because to be a great lawyer one must be able to understand the nuances of the many people with whom he deals. My deceased friend was a generalist. He could deal with anyone about anything. I will miss him greatly.

ક્ષેત્ર ક્ષેત્ર ક્ષેત્ર

# Supreme Court Sit-In Case

As I WRITE THIS essay, demonstrations are taking place in a number of Islamic countries. Demonstrators who are risking their lives, and in some cases losing them, are seeking freedom from despotic governments that are as willing to kill them as look at them. I am awestruck that people have such courage. Then I remember that I once met such a person, shared an office with him and dropped him off on the way home. The demonstrators in countries thousands of miles away make me remember that I was privileged to have known such a person, right here in our nation's capital.

When I was in law school I worked as a law clerk in the U.S. Department of Justice. After graduation and admission to the bar I continued in the Department as a lawyer. The Justice Department's building was overcrowded at that time, so lawyers shared offices. Of several possibilities I chose the lawyer who was the quietest and most self-contained. My office mate, from a rural parish in Louisiana and black as coal, spoke little and maintained an aura of dignity at all times. Even on swelteringly hot days when my wife and I dropped him off on our way home, he kept his suit jacket on and never loosened his shirt collar or necktie.

When he was ready to leave the Department of Justice, my office mate decided to seek employment with a large national corporation that had never previously hired a black lawyer. After several trips to its offices, where he knew he had been carefully scrutinized, he told me he believed that a job offer was possible. As he did with every document, my office mate labored diligently over the employment application.

One afternoon, after a long period of silent work, my office mate looked up and asked me how I thought he should answer a particular question. The question, a customary one, was whether the applicant had ever been convicted of a crime other than a minor traffic offense. As he asked the question, my office mate handed me a volume of the United States Reports, open to the first page of the Supreme Court's decision declaring segregated lunch counters unconstitutional. There, in footnote 1, which lists the cases the Supreme Court addressed in its decision, was a case in which the State of Louisiana had convicted my office mate for sitting at a lunch counter reserved for whites. "Is this *you*?" I asked him. The answer was yes, that it was my office mate, one of the most reserved and peaceful men I have ever met. I was looking at a black man who had the courage during the years of segregation to sit at a whites-only lunch counter in Louisiana. I don't need to see television footage of demonstrators in distant countries to know there are people of such courage in this world. I've known one.*

*Awestruck on learning what my office mate had done, I tried to think of other instances when I was similarly overwhelmed. Although I have met and occasionally represented people famous for their accomplishments in public office or sports or the arts, I have never been overwhelmed by them. After much thought, I could think of only one instance when I was as moved by the presence of a person as by my office mate's. One summer, while my family was eating dinner at a resort hotel in Long Island, an unremarkable-looking man wearing a red blazer recognized my stepfather and walked over to our table. "Jonas, I'd like to introduce you to my family," my stepfather said, and, turning to us, said, "this is Dr. Jonas Salk." I couldn't believe it. The man who had eradicated polio, the most dreaded disease in my lifetime, was standing next to our dinner table exchanging remarks with my stepfather.

᠍᠍ ᠍᠍ ᠍᠍

# New Expert in Construction Case

A PARTNER AND I prepared for the trial of a complex construction case. The foundation of an office building had become defective and our client was the contractor whose company had built it. The owner of the building, the general contractor, the architect, the structural engineer, and the soils analyst were also parties to the lawsuit. The question was which party was responsible for the defective foundation. Our client contended that it had done the work properly and that the defect was due to some combination of the work of the architect, the structural engineer, and the soils analyst. We intended to show that the plans provided to our client, who had followed them slavishly, were defective. Our expert was prepared to say that if the plans had been correct, the foundation would have supported the building.

I was never completely comfortable with the expert we were planning to use even though on paper his qualifications were superb. In fact, he had developed the particular type of foundation that was used. Less than a week before trial, my misgivings grew to the point that I thought about our expert constantly. My problem was that he was an effete intellectual in professor's clothes, thus not the sort of person the average juror finds trustworthy. What we needed was a "high boots" expert with dirt under his fingernails from supervising the construction of foundations. When I told my partner my misgivings about our expert, he agreed. Our problem was how to obtain a new expert, prepare that expert, and file the required legal documents within the four or five business days remaining before trial.

It took almost a full day to identify a new expert. We wanted someone who supervised the construction of the type of foundation in our case. We telephoned six or eight of the best candidates, but all of them were unavailable for one reason or another. Finally, as a result of what can only be characterized as shameless begging, a very experienced foundation construction supervisor who was working on a building in Pennsylvania agreed to talk to us. Our understanding was that we would go to a hotel near the construction site where he was working and meet him in the evening after he finished work.

Our new expert, Sam Milstead, looked letter-perfect. He was wearing stained brown corduroys, a pullover shirt with large permanent stains under the arms and work boots. He was carrying a hard hat. We made arrangements for his testimony and spent some of our client's money to do so. Our "high boots" expert was going to come to Baltimore to testify. After Sam had reviewed the plans and learned what had occurred, he delivered the perfect script:

> The problem, you see, is that these plans call for expulsion of the bulbs on the PIFs [pressure injected footings] at the wrong level. Since PIFs are not grounded on bedrock like steel columns, the bulbs must be expelled at a level that offers sufficient bearing capacity. If the ground around the bulb is too soft or sandy, it will not provide sufficient support for the PIFs. Once you know the weight of the building, you can determine how much each PIF must support and then determine the best place to expel the bulbs. These bulbs were expelled far too near the surface. Your guys followed the plans, but someone in the design team blew it big time.

When I called the former expert to tell him his testimony would no longer be needed, I was glad he didn't ask me why. I wouldn't have been comfortable telling him that at the last minute we realized what should have been obvious to us much sooner.

❧ ❧ ❧

# A Dishonest Witness

I INTERVIEWED A YOUNG man with an investigator I knew well. We planned to use him as a witness at a forthcoming trial. He would be a valuable witness, but not indispensable. He told us about his family, where he had gone to high school, that he attended Harvard College and had worked at several interesting jobs.

The young man had worked for the company involved in our case for about two years after college. His history seemed credible and we quickly turned to the details of his work with the company. We spent a good deal of time clarifying specific details of his work and putting important facts into chronological order. The interview lasted nearly three hours and at the end we told the young man we wanted to interview him once more before trial.

My investigator, Warren Bittner, never believed anything until he had verified it. Unbeknownst to me, Warren checked the young man's background and learned he had never attended Harvard College. I was surprised by this finding since the educational background of our potential witness made absolutely no difference. People generally mislead others about background facts in ways that would do them some good.

Warren and I scheduled an appointment with the young man for about a week later to reinterview him. Our plan was to go through his background with him again, indicating we wanted to be certain we understood everything correctly. The young man reiterated his earlier statements exactly, Harvard College included. At this point Warren interrupted him and told him he had checked with the registrar at Harvard and learned that he never attended. "The registrar's mistaken," the young man said, "I attended Harvard from 1997 to 2001. I was a sociology major and had a good grade average."

"Tell us some of the courses you took and who taught them," Warren asked.

"I don't remember things like that very well, but my transcript would answer your question."

Our potential witness had answers to other questions, about where he lived while attending Harvard, friends with whom he socialized, and memorable aspects of his college years. At no time did he appear embarrassed or in any way retreat from what he had told us about Harvard. After we had asked all our questions and exhausted our efforts to get him to change his story, we reluctantly concluded that the young man believed what he told us. He had created a fictional experience for his own purposes. We didn't use him as a witness.

ॐ ॐ ॐ

# Country Justice

I'VE TRIED MANY CASES and argued many appeals in federal and state courts, but I learned something important about justice when I handled a case involving a traffic ticket—the only traffic ticket case I've ever had.

A federal agent with whom I dealt regularly came to me one day and asked if I would help him with a "little matter." The little matter was a speeding ticket he had received while on federal business in a rural county in northern Maryland. Although technically able to do so, state police generally avoid ticketing federal agents working in their area. Special Agent Douglas Wethersby had received a ticket for driving 54 miles per hour in a 35-miles-per-hour zone.

Doug didn't want the ticket on his record and asked me if I would accompany him to court. I agreed and we decided to have lunch on the way back.

The traffic court was near several military reservations, and when we arrived we learned it was close to one of them. Entering the courtroom we saw that the judge was already seated at the bench and a large crowd was sitting on folding chairs around the room. We took seats at the back and waited our turn.

As we waited we saw that after each case was decided the judge spoke openly to everyone in the courtroom, explaining his decision. The crowd listened attentively to what he was saying. These are the sort of remarks the judge made:

> The reason I decided that Mrs. Spencer should not be convicted of this violation was that she was rushing to the hospital to see her son. Although Officer Stanton certainly was correct in ticketing her for speeding, the circumstances of this case, which anyone can understand, warranted this result. In general, excuses for speeding don't work in court. This circumstance was unusual and so I made an exception for that reason.

The judge was not required to provide such explanations and most of the people in the courtroom wouldn't remember them. As I listened to the judge's explanations, however, I realized that something important was occurring. The people in the courtroom learned that the law was reasonable and that judges did not decide cases on an arbitrary basis. For many in that room this may have been their only experience in court. Many cases were heard and explained before the clerk called for Doug's case. Doug and the officer who had ticketed him took their places in front of the bench and told the judge their stories. I stood next to Doug and had nothing to say other than to introduce myself.

Surprised, the judge remarked in a friendly manner that it was unusual to have a federal prosecutor representing someone in traffic court. Although I have always felt I did not make my point as strongly as I wanted to, I told the judge that being present in his courtroom and hearing what he said after each case was a privilege.

The judge determined that a federal agent on duty should not have received a traffic ticket from a state police officer. As he explained to those in the courtroom, the conduct of federal business could not be curtailed by the state. This did not necessarily justify Doug's speeding, but everyone who heard the judge's explanation understood the reason for his decision. Doug and I had a lot to talk about when we stopped for lunch on our way back.

ૐ ૐ ૐ

# Depravity: Lindbergh Act Case

I HAVE BEEN INVOLVED in cases of armed bank robbery, a few homicides, sexual abuse and other types of violence, but I have only once witnessed depravity on the scale of someone like Charles Manson or Timothy McVeigh.

Years ago I prosecuted a Lindbergh Act kidnaping case. The three defendants planned a robbery at the home of a young woman holding a dinner party. After they had obtained what they wanted and were preparing to leave, the leader of the group decided to take one of the young women from the party with them. For approximately 12 hours the three men held her and committed every imaginable violent sexual act on their victim.

The crime took place in a rented truck, which the trio drove across state lines, thus conferring federal jurisdiction. In the morning, exhausted and finished with their victim, the men dumped her out of the truck and shot her through the abdomen as she lay in the street. The bullet ricocheted off the asphalt and entered her body a second time. Grievously injured and bleeding profusely, the young woman crawled along the street screaming for help. Amazingly, she lived to testify at trial.

For procedural reasons, the leader of the group was tried separately. The trial took place before a federal judge for whom I had great respect and a diversified jury. Unfortunately, the judge's courtroom was unusually small for a federal courtroom and the prosecutor's table was unusually close to the defendant's table. Despite my best efforts, I saw the defendant's face from the corner of my eye during most of the trial.

Preparing the victim to testify was an experience I never want to repeat. She was married at that time and her husband and I decided he would remain outside the courtroom while she testified. Her testimony about what she had experienced was shocking and excruciatingly painful. On several occasions everyone in the courtroom was fighting back tears and the courageous young woman broke down entirely. The judge granted every request for a recess I made during her testimony.

An hour or so into her testimony, as she struggled to explain the details of her nightmare, the doors to the courtroom opened and two men, obviously friends of the defendant, entered and sat at the back of the courtroom. I saw the defendant turn 90 degrees in his seat and I saw a broad grin come across his face and the flash of a gold tooth. I saw him give a high sign to his friends. I saw a man who could listen to the testimony of a young woman on whom he had inflicted immeasurable suffering and smile with self-satisfaction. At that moment I saw depravity.

The jury didn't spend much time finding the defendant guilty. When he was sentenced several weeks later, the judge imposed a life sentence and told the defendant he had never known anyone to engage in more evil conduct.

For various reasons the death penalty wasn't available in this case. I have often asked myself whether I would have requested it. Although I will never know for certain, I believe I would have requested the judge to order this man's life ended. The broad grin and high sign during the victim's courageous effort to tell of her agony would, I believe, have made it possible for me to be instrumental in ending a life.

᪄ ᪄ ᪄

# Conviction of a Vice President

I WAS NOTHING MORE than a spectator in this case, yet I remember it as vividly as if I had been a participant. It was 1973 and the case involved the criminal conviction of a Vice President of the United States.

Three of seventeen prosecutors in the United States Attorney's Office in Baltimore worked on the case of Spiro T. Agnew for several years. A Special Agent of the Internal Revenue Service was assigned to work with them. From its inception through the day Vice President Agnew was convicted, the three prosecutors did not discuss the case with anyone. I did my usual work as a prosecutor during the entire Agnew investigation.

The day I remember vividly is the day the Vice President was convicted. It began when Elliot Richardson, Attorney General of the United States, arrived at our offices. The Attorney General walked down the corridor containing the United States Attorney's Office, sticking his head in each prosecutor's office to say that something extraordinary was about to happen in the courtroom of a senior judge at the rear of the courthouse. The Attorney General told us that seats in the jury box had been reserved for prosecutors. It seemed strange to me that what was going to be a major event was not taking place in the much larger ceremonial courtroom in the center of the courthouse.

My colleagues and I went directly to the courtroom and took seats in the jury box. I wound up in seat No. 1, the seat where a jury foreperson customarily sits. From there I could see all the way down the corridor that led to the courtroom. The seats in the spectator portion of the courtroom were rapidly filling with people who had apparently been alerted to what was occurring. Some were members of the press I recognized. Only a few minutes passed before two men in dark suits walked side by side down the corridor to the courtroom. They were the Vice President of the United States and his lawyer, Judah Best.

When they entered the courtroom the Vice President promptly stood in front of the seat designated for defendants. His lawyer stood in front of the seat designated for defense lawyers. The Attorney General, the United States Attorney, and my three colleagues assembled in the place designated for prosecutors. As always, the prosecutor's table was located closer to the jury box than the defense lawyer's table.

Because every federal judge in Maryland had some acquaintance with Spiro Agnew, a former Governor of Maryland, a judge from Virginia was to preside. I did not recognize him as he took his seat behind the bench. The case of *United States v. Spiro T. Agnew* was called immediately and the participants performed their functions as in any ordinary federal criminal case. The Vice President entered a plea of *nolo contendere* (no contest) to one charge of tax evasion, although he had also been charged with extortion, bribery and conspiracy. The prosecutors recited the facts, the Vice President admitted the facts were correct, and his plea was accepted.

In ordinary cases sentencing takes place after several weeks and a pre-sentence report is prepared. In the Vice President's case, sentencing took place immediately. He was not sentenced to a term of incarceration but was ordered to pay a fine. He had resigned the vice presidency prior to his appearance in court. Several years later I learned from a knowledgeable person that the Virginia judge who presided over the case knew in advance that the prosecutors would not recommend incarceration. I was told that the judge had difficulty accepting the bargain.

The Vice President and his lawyer left the courtroom immediately after the proceeding was concluded. Media representatives made futile attempts to speak with them as they departed. It was clear that Vice President Agnew and his lawyer had decided to be in public view for the shortest possible time.

What I most remember about the case of Vice President Agnew is my discomfort with the places of the people in the courtroom. I was accustomed to courtrooms packed with spectators and media representatives so that aspect of the case did not affect me. What kept going through my mind was the strangeness of seeing the Vice President of the United States in the place reserved for criminal defendants. It was strange to see the lawyer for the Vice President standing where defense lawyers customarily stood. In addition, the prosecutors included the Attorney General of the United States, the United States Attorney and the Assistant United States Attorneys who had worked on the case. In place of the judge who customarily presided in the courtroom was an unfamiliar judge. I was seated in the place where the jury foreperson usually sat. My usual seat was at the prosecutor's table. I had tried many cases in the courtroom where this case took place, and the deviations from the customary locations of participants was difficult to accept. A Vice President of the United States is not supposed to be the defendant in a criminal case. My recollection of the criminal conviction of Vice President Spiro Agnew is surreal even after all these years.

### Plea for Mercy

ONCE IN A WHILE a seemingly insignificant moment stands out in my memory of a case like a mountain rising from a plain. It is always the same. It is always a moment when a flash of humanity, of grace really, punctuates the inexorable formality of legal procedures.

Years ago when I was a prosecutor, while driving to work I heard on the morning news that a Romanian fishing vessel had been arrested by the Coast Guard for illegally fishing in the Contiguous Fishing Zone. The vessel was being brought to Baltimore for security reasons and would arrive in a few hours. I knew the file would be on my desk when I arrived.

I learned quickly that the ship was owned by a government corporation and, therefore, essentially by the country of Romania. To complicate things, the U.S. Secretary of Commerce was at that time in Bucharest, the capital city, negotiating the extension of a bilateral treaty. The Soviet Union was still intact at that time and the so-called "Iron Curtain" countries had only tenuous relationships with the United States, making this case rife with possibilities for political involvement. In fact, these never occurred.

When the ship arrived in Baltimore I learned that it was a new, technologically advanced fishing vessel manufactured in Poland and containing, in addition to a crew of dozens of men, two Polish engineers from the manufacturer.

I had a lot to do before the initial hearing, scheduled for later that day. I advised the Romanian Consul in Washington of the situation and told him that he or his designee was free to attend all proceedings. The Vice Consul dispatched to Baltimore proved to be an obsequious little man who followed me in and out of the courthouse like a puppy. I next obtained an English–Romanian translator from the language school of a local university. I spoke with the federal public defender assigned to represent the Romanians until they could procure their own lawyer. I also contacted one of only two prosecutors in the country who had ever had such a case. From him I learned that such cases involve a civil case against the vessel itself and a criminal case against its captain.

The Romanians engaged a lawyer about a week later. He was an excellent lawyer whom I knew from earlier dealings. He told me soon after he was engaged that the captain of the fishing vessel would almost certainly receive harsh treatment when he returned to Romania. He was considered responsible for the ship's having been caught in the Contiguous Fishing Zone and for the cases against the vessel and the captain. His possible penalties in Romania, I was told, included loss of his status as a captain and incarceration. When the Deputy Director of Immigration decided to permit the vessel's crew limited rights to leave the ship, every crew member except the captain took advantage of the opportunity.

While the case was proceeding, the lawyer for the Romanians asked me if I would like to see the ship. He told me I would be impressed by its technological devices. I accepted my colleague's offer and shortly thereafter we visited the ship at its mooring several blocks from my office. A few of the crew members nodded to us as we crossed the gangplank, but aside from that we were greeted largely with indifference. The technological devices were indeed impressive. They included special fins on the rear of the ship to capture schools of fish, an elaborate control room on the bridge, and a freezing room below deck to store the catch.

After we had seen these, my colleague asked me if I would like to see the captain's quarters. We walked down a short corridor to the captain's small stateroom, which was neatly furnished and well equipped. When we entered his stateroom the captain, dressed in pressed and fresh-looking clothing, was standing and he bowed his head towards us. He appeared to be in his early thirties. He spoke no English. My colleague and I had a little conversation about the stateroom and then, with gestures, the captain offered us drinks consisting of wine and club soda. My colleague accepted his offer and, although I probably should not have, I accepted it as well.

We stood next to the captain's nightstand as we sipped our drinks and stared at one another. Then I caught a detail I will never forget. There was a square machine, approximately one foot by one foot in size, on top of the nightstand. I did not know its purpose but its top was clearly slippery. Sitting there, in a small, ornate gold frame, was a photograph of what was obviously the captain's wife and two children. I recall my reaction on seeing the picture. It was that the captain had placed the picture there in expectation of our seeing it. The picture could never have been kept on a slippery surface within a rocking ship on the high seas. By putting it within our view the captain was telling us, telling me as the prosecutor, that he had a family back in Romania who would share whatever suffering was inflicted on him.

I can see that picture in my mind's eye today, sitting on the slippery top of the machine on the captain's nightstand. I can see the frightened young man who bowed his head and could not speak our language to tell us what he wanted us to know. I can see him standing next to his night-stand as we drank the drinks he had given us.

Now, many years later when I think about the case, I have no particular feelings about the legal matters that were addressed. I have no particular feelings about the vessel that was brought to Baltimore. I have no particular feelings about the court hearings or the extensive publicity the case received. What I remember with crystal clarity is the captain standing next to his nightstand on which a picture of his wife and children was placed on a slippery surface. "I have a family," the picture told me, "be merciful."

# CHAPTER THREE

# Reflections

## Preface

A GREAT DEAL OF every lawyer's time is devoted to thinking. In many cases lawyers spend at least as much time thinking as they do meeting with clients and others, drafting documents, arguing legal points and other active work. If a lawyer does not spend thinking time well, it is very doubtful that anything that lawyer does will be useful to clients.

I do not know where their mental wanderings take other lawyers. For me, thinking about cases often causes me to think about how law interacts with other disciplines. I would have to confess that I often lose track of the case I am working on, at least for a time.

In the reflections that follow I will tell of instances in which my thinking has brought law into contact with painting, music, architecture, money, ethics and scientific disciplines such as neuroscience. I will offer some thoughts on how the practice of law fits into a broader social context. Since it is my opinion that there is no discipline or matter of social concern that does not somehow touch the matter of law, my musings may be a little too expansive for some readers. I can only say that as with every aspect of this book, the following reflections are true to my own experience and not clever contrivances to fill these pages.

What I am seeking to convey in these reflections is a sense of the feelings that have arisen in various cases. As I said in the Introduction to this book, it is a misconception, albeit understandable, that lawyers do their work without passion. I hope these reflections will help explain why this is not so.

ᘏ ᘏ ᘏ

# Depositions on Friday

THE DEPOSITIONS ARE RUNNING late this Friday afternoon. My client, a graying surgeon in the seat next to me, is nearly asleep. I put my hand on his knee as he begins to snore.

My client's deposition has been taken. The witness now is a nurse who was in the recovery room at the hospital where his patient died of "aspiration of vomitus," choking on your own puke, after my client removed his patient's inflamed gallbladder. The issue is whether the post-operative care of the deceased forty-eight year old husband, father and breadwinner met prevailing medical standards. The plaintiff's lawyer is keenly focused as he questions the recovery room nurse. He knows she is the key to obtaining big money from the deep-pocket hospital.

Questioning continues while street lights go on outside our conference room. People are leaving work to go to restaurants and parties. The stenographer at the end of the table raises her hand to signal she must insert a new roll of paper.

"Would you agree, Ms. Clark, that when Mr. Olmstead arrived in the recovery room after surgery he was at risk for aspiration?"

"Every postoperative patient is at risk for aspiration."

"And that would include Mr. Olmstead?"

"Yes."

I can hear the forthcoming questions before the plaintiff's lawyer asks them. They will concern the hospital's procedures for addressing the risks of postoperative aspiration, whether they were observed or not observed, the hazards of failure to observe them. The plaintiff's lawyer, whose thumb and forefinger surround his necktie and move up and down it in masturbatory fashion, will direct the nurse's attention to the fact that postoperative patients, groggy from anesthesia, may be unable to expel vomit. He will question her about the risk of aspiration presented by a supine patient, the need for constant monitoring and suction, the advice and admonitions of medical authorities.

Suddenly, I hear something else. It is music! It is Bach's *B-Minor Mass*. I can hear valveless trumpets, their glorious warbling just free enough of constant pitch. My favorite chorus, *Osanna in Excelsis*, is beginning.

"What procedures, if any, Ms. Clark, does your hospital observe in the recovery room to address the risk of postoperative aspiration?"

"We monitor each patient in the recovery room closely. We have suction available at each patient's bedside."

I am no longer listening to the nurse's carefully rehearsed answers. I know the script by heart. Every lawyer in the room knows it.

I am straining to hear the music, thinking of the time I attended the Bach Festival. In its performance of the *B-Minor Mass*, each member of the orchestra and chorus displayed more passion than all the desiccated husks gathered around the conference table will expend on this entire case.

"What steps are taken, Ms. Clark, when a postoperative patient in the recovery room aspirates?"

"The overriding concern when that occurs is to be certain that the airway remains open. Proper positioning of the patient and use of suction to clear the throat are the most important things. In Mr. Olmstead's case, we. . . ."

The music interrupts her. Bach's magnificence is now in counterpoint with the questions and answers. The deposition has lost its mock urgency. The lawyers are like retired soldiers still wearing their uniforms.

Now it is totally dark outside. The last frantic rays of sun have vanished from the faceless glass building next door. Lawyers and secretaries are leaving our building. I can see them enter the street below.

Our conference room has become a hermetic chamber, its occupants enslaved by tedium. For an instant my client awakens, stares rabbit-like at the witness, then returns to sleep. The lawyers are barely feigning interest. One of them leans to the left in an effort to pass gas silently, which does not succeed.

"Did there come a time, Ms. Clark, when you or any member of the recovery room staff saw any indication that Mr. Olmstead's airway was obstructed?"

"An hour or so after Mr. Olmstead arrived in the recovery room, his blood gas analysis showed oxygen saturation below the normal level."

"What is the meaning of blood gas oxygen saturation below the normal level?"

But no one cares. The questions and answers are no longer the melody. They are an obbligato, a steady unengaging cadence below it. The shrill exchanges between lawyers that punctuated the depositions with objections "for the record" have ended. The unashamed pretense of concern for the death of a man is over. The objective is simply to finish and leave.

"What significance, if any, do you attach, Ms. Clark, to Mr. Olmstead's being in a supine position at the time in question?"

The nurse answers with the text drummed into her by her attorney. The lawyers around the table all but ignore her. The stenographer pounds her stenograph in a state of near hypnosis. My client sleeps peacefully in the seat beside me.

Bach's music surrounds me now. I can see the chorus holding their scores in front of them. I can hear their rising voices reverberate from the high walls of the chapel. I am no longer confined to this ritual in Conference Room B, "Reserved for Depositions" and strewn with documents, yellow legal pads and empty coffee cups. I am outside in the night, moving freely, as in a song.

à❧ à❧ à❧

# The Whole Truth

THIS MORNING I'M MAKING the truth.

Yes, you heard it right. I didn't say I'm finding the truth or telling the truth. I said exactly what I mean: I'm making the truth.

I don't mean, of course, that I'm lying. If I were, surely I wouldn't admit it here. What I'm doing is the somewhat convoluted thing lawyers do every day. I'm selecting from myriad facts and details those that can be fit together seamlessly to present a picture of the matter that best suits my client's needs. The so-called "limits of advocacy" prohibit a lawyer from offering untrue facts, but they don't curtail a lawyer's freedom to select and arrange facts in any particular manner.

The client for whom I'm working has violated the spirit, if not the letter, of a contract he made with his employer. He persuaded clients of his employer, an accounting firm, to patronize a new firm he was start-ing. He surreptitiously copied records of the accounting firm for use in his new practice. He opened his new office directly across the street from his former employer's office. There's no question that the whole truth of the matter does not bode well for my client.

When this sort of thing occurs I think of the oath witnesses are required to take: "I do solemnly swear [or affirm] that the testimony I am about to give shall be the truth, the whole truth and nothing but the truth." Lawyers don't take a similar oath about their work. If they did, the legal profession would come to a full stop. Lawyers must tell the truth and nothing but the truth, but they are not required to tell the whole truth. Lawyers are advocates for clients and in a case such as the one I'm working on the whole truth doesn't help my client. The whole truth in this case would be that my client has wantonly violated his contract with his employer and, if justice were to prevail, he would be required to pay for it.

My client's greatest fear is not that the court will require him to pay damages to his former employer. My client's new practice is lucrative and he can afford to pay for what he has done. My client's greatest fear is that the court will enjoin him from conducting his new practice. This would be devastating.

There's no way I can make the truth be that my client didn't violate his contract. The alchemy of selection and reorganization of facts and details cannot be stretched that far. Since there's no arguable view of what occurred that affords my client any sympathy, I decide to base my case on showing what an injunction would do to my client's clients.

My client and I review his clients and select three who require particularly personal services by an accountant familiar with their businesses. These clients are not representative of all the clients he served while he worked for his former employer. The lawyer's exemption from the whole-truth requirement permits me to select the best candidates for the point I want to make. My point is that an injunction would disrupt long-term accountant–client relationships and therefore would not be in the best interests of the clients.

I must live with the burden of knowing that I am making the truth in a different form from what a neutral person would find it to be. This is a burden I accept, but not without reservation. My reservation is that the better I am at what I'm doing, the harder I work, the stronger advocate I become, the more I'm making a truth that isn't representative of the whole truth. I wonder sometimes if the image of lawyers as charlatans doesn't arise because we make the truth for clients.

## Where Have All the Books Gone?

YEARS AGO I AGREED to brief and argue an appeal in a criminal case that another lawyer had tried. When I read the trial transcript there didn't appear to be much hope for my client. The only issue of possible merit, fortunately preserved by the trial attorney, was whether my client's conviction violated the constitutional proscription against double jeopardy. My client's conduct had been the subject of a previous conviction for another offense. Since our law firm was new at the time and had only a small library, I visited a larger library nearby.

Ever since law school law libraries have been indescribably attractive to me. The long rows of shelves containing cases and comments in handsomely bound books are a fitting repository for the majesty of the law. The long wood tables, at one of which I selected a seat, invite critical thinking and interesting work. As I sat down I noticed across the table a pile of books, some open to particular pages, on top of which was a note saying "DO NOT DISTURB."

It didn't take long to determine that the controlling authority in the double jeopardy question was a Supreme Court opinion, *Blockburger v. United States*.[1] The Supreme Court had held that the double jeopardy prohibition is not violated by a second prosecution if each of the two offenses requires at least one fact not required by the other. Although it was difficult to understand the reason for the second prosecution of my client, a reading of the two statutes clearly established a separate fact in each offense. The progeny of *Blockburger* (which included an opinion by Justice Felix Frankfurter, *Gore v. United States*[2]), which I searched in vain, provided no safe harbor for my client. I was confronted with every lawyer's recurrent dilemma: a position in which I believed, but as to which the law showed no generosity.

An hour or so into my work the person using the pile of books across the table returned. He was a lawyer I had encountered once or twice, but did not know well. We exchanged greetings and my colleague quickly got to work, continuing his notes on the yellow legal pad he extracted from his attaché case. In casual remarks over the next half hour, my colleague and I learned what the other was working on. His matter concerned a

---

[1] 284 U.S. 299 (1932).
[2] 357 U.S. 386 (1958).

summary judgment motion with an interesting twist in one of the sup-
porting affidavits. We exchanged comments about our respective projects
and about our practices. I explained I was working on a double jeopardy
case where both prosecutions grew out of the same situation but each
offense contained a separate factual requirement.

After a while I said, "Can I run this by you?" To be honest, I was
more interested in learning how my argument sounded to another lawyer
than in receiving his opinion. "Isn't it implicit in *Blockburger* that the separate facts be empirically meaningful in the incident that took place?"
Although I didn't at first realize it, the argument I would ultimately make
was taking shape. I suppose I was following the old adage that when the
facts are not good you argue the law and when the law isn't good you
argue the facts. I decided to argue the facts and it worked! The successful
case is known as *Thomas v. State*.[3] We had added a new wrinkle to the
*Blockburger* "required evidence test."

I can not dissect the things that affected the evolution of my thinking in this case. Surely the environment in which I was working contributed in some way. Surely the assemblage of books in front of me
played a part. My exchanges with my colleague contributed as well. I am
sure of only one thing: no one sitting in an office alone tapping keys and
looking at a computer screen could be in an environment as hospitable
to legal research as I was that day.

Readers must be thinking by now that there isn't much to this story.
But for one thing, I would agree. Going to a library to do research and
chatting with a colleague is certainly not a plot for the next John
Grisham novel. The only notable thing about this story is that most
lawyers who embarked upon their practices less than ten or fifteen years
ago will never have such an experience. Computerized research has obvi-
ated the need for books and libraries.

Although not intended to do so, computerized research has also
largely foreclosed serendipitous research discoveries and casual encounters with colleagues. Many of us have a storehouse of legal knowledge we
acquired turning the pages of law books and in banter with other lawyers.
Sometimes turning pages you will pass by a case that relates to a matter
for another client. Sometimes a case will catch your eye simply because
it interests you. Even in the laborious process of Shepardization (seeing
where a case has been cited) you may learn something by seeing how
seminal opinions have radiated to other courts.

---

[3] 277 Md. 257 (1976).

We live in an age where the advantages of technology are celebrated to a fare-thee-well, and computerized legal research certainly has advantages. A single practitioner in the smallest town in North Dakota can now perform the same legal research as a lawyer in a large firm in Manhattan. Lawyers with computers are able to do legal research virtually anywhere at any time. Computerized research eliminates the cost of law books (which I can remember purchasing from a retiring federal judge), floor space and structural requirements of law libraries, the necessity for librarians and the inevitable delays installing supplements. I doubt if anyone will miss hearing people walking through the halls shouting things like, "Does anybody know where I can find 283 F.2d?"

But the case for law books does not rest on notions of efficiency. In terms of efficiency the case for law books is lost. In a profession that increasingly measures itself in terms of quantities—salaries, expenses, billable hours, cut-to-the-chase time requirements—the value of books and libraries is disregarded. In the process, we are losing the best of practicing law: the richness of the terrain it covers, its endless intellectual stimulation, and the opportunities it provides for rewarding interactions with colleagues. There are professions in which such losses may be regrettable, but not devastating. In the practice of law, however, technology appears to have streamlined the architecture of our work by performing a brilliant operation in which the patient has died.

๒ะ ๒ะ ๒ะ

# Conflicts of Interest

I HAVE A PROBLEM with my client, Harold Sturdevan. Harold builds shopping centers and I hate them. I believe shopping centers eviscerate communities, manifest aesthetic bankruptcy, and promote social pathologies. As Harold sits in my conference room with his latest set of plans and simplistic pro forma, I wonder whether I have the sort of conflict of interest that precludes my working for him.

The treatment of legal ethics in law schools is superficial. Students are taught that they must avoid conflicts of interest but are advised only of obvious ones. Every lawyer knows it would be a conflict of interest to represent the plaintiff and the defendant in a lawsuit or the seller and the purchaser in a sale or the lender and the borrower in a loan. The situation with Harold, however, is not readily apparent. The conflict of interest is invisible. No one can see that I abhor my client's projects.

The reason conflicts of interest are prohibited is that they are believed to dampen a lawyer's enthusiasm. When a conflict of interest is obvious, this is not difficult to understand. When a conflict of interest is not obvious, as in my situation with Harold, I am the only person aware of it.

Conflicts of interest are often cured by a lawyer's advising the client of his other interest and obtaining his client's consent to work for him notwithstanding it. In my imagination, but surely not in reality, I consider this possibility. I imagine advising Harold of my conflict of interest and seeking his consent in this colloquy:

"Harold, I must tell you before we turn to the finance and leasing documents for your new shopping center that I profoundly dislike shopping centers. I must advise you of that possible conflict of interest and ask whether you want me to continue working for you."

Harold might answer me in two different ways:

"I understand, and frankly I don't care what you think about shopping centers. If you do the documents correctly, you can go home and wish I was dead."

Or

"If that's how you feel, why the hell do you want to work for a shopping center developer? I'm going to switch to a lawyer who doesn't hate what I do."

Neither answer would be particularly attractive. The first answer reduces me to an implement with feelings that make no difference. The second results in my losing a client.

The only way I can think of to solve my problem would be to tell Harold that I made a mistake when I agreed to work for him. I would explain the basis of my mistake, and my explanation would obviously offend him. My conclusion is that it wouldn't be desirable for me to advise Harold of my feelings about his work.

Lawyers generally keep their mouths shut when something about a client is offensive to them. A lawyer may be offended by the personal aspects of a client or, as in Harold's case, the nature of his work. Lawyers have likes and dislikes just as everyone else does, and it's disquieting to think of how many clients are served by lawyers who have invisible conflicts of interest. I wonder if many clients think about this possibility.

I'll return to the conference room where Harold is sitting and give my full attention to his documents. I'll do a good job for Harold and he will never know how I feel about his work.

⁂ ⁂ ⁂

# Integrity

MY FAMILY HAS OWNED a small house in eastern Long Island for many years. We use it primarily in the summer but occasionally go there at other times. The master bedroom of the house had no bathroom and, after many years, we decided to add one. A contractor we had known for a long time did the work and he hired the plumber and the electrician. There was one part of the job, however, that the contractor was unable to do. We needed someone to do the tile work.

The tile job was so small that most contractors didn't want it. Finally, at a friend's recommendation, we found a contractor who agreed to do the job over the winter, when business was slow. We agreed on a price and left a few boxes of the tiles we had selected in the bathroom. We also left a bag of powder which was to be used to make the grout.

The understanding was that a neighbor would let the contractor into the house and we would come to see the work within a week or two after it was finished. Things did not go as planned that winter and we never made the trip to see the finished work. Since our failure to inspect the work was due to our own difficulties, I paid the contractor for the work before seeing it. If I had a client who did that, I would give that client a lawyer's scolding.

When we arrived at the house late the following spring I went immediately to the new bathroom to see the tile work. I was amazed by what I saw. The contractor had done a perfect job. Where there were difficult angles in the small room, he had cut and installed odd-shaped pieces of tile perfectly. Where the floor was at an angle to permit water to run down the shower drain, he had flawlessly conformed the tiles to the proper slope. The grout in every space between tiles was uniformly just below the surface of the tiles. In addition, the bathroom was spotless. The contractor had placed the extra tiles and grout in the basement in the very place we would have put them had we been there.

It was not simply the excellence of the contractor's work that so impressed me. It was also that he had done the work with no one watching over him or even being nearby. I'm sure the contractor knew that a merely passable job would have resulted in payment of the agreed price.

I could conclude only that pride and self-respect are probably appropriate descriptions of what motivated him.

Seeing his work has made me ask myself more than once whether I have as much integrity as he does. My brief call to him to thank him for his excellent work didn't come close to expressing everything I felt about him.

ੋ ੋ ੋ

# Small Town Lawyer

MY OFFICE HAS BEEN in a high-rise office building in the middle of a large city as long as I've practiced law. I've commuted to and from an underground garage on an interstate highway often clogged with traffic and always unpleasant to drive. My choice of workplace, or more accurately its use as a result of non-choice, has been one of the greatest mistakes of my life. To say I have hated, even dreaded, the days and nights I have spent in my office does not fully capture the effect doing so has had upon me. It is accurate to say that my office betrays the person I know myself to be. It requires me to suppress—no, to disregard—a lifelong yearning so urgent that it is atavistic. I don't know when my feelings about small towns arose, but I cannot remember not having them.

The matter I am working on is simple. It is a garden-variety negligence case against my client, the owner of a hardware store. The case involves a minor injury to a customer who contends he cut himself on a lawnmower blade in the store. Since my client carries considerable insurance for such claims, my only responsibility is to ensure that the man who is suing him doesn't receive an award exceeding the insurance coverage. The chance of this occurring is roughly equal to the chance that I will learn how to fly by tomorrow.

My job today is to attend the deposition of the man claiming injury and be certain the lawyer provided by the insurance company covers everything that should be covered. The injured man, who can barely locate the minuscule scar on his finger, has arrived for the deposition at his lawyer's office in a converted house on the North Shore of Long Island. He has forgotten to bring with him the records he claims show the time he lost at work because of the injury.

It will take the plaintiff a little over an hour to return to his place of business, retrieve the records he forgot to bring, and return to the deposition. Since there's nothing for the lawyers and the stenographer to do until he returns, we decide to get some air in front of the office. It is a pleasant fall day and we engage in informal conversation to pass the time. Down the street from where we are gathered are a few small stores, a gas station, and private houses, some of them converted to offices.

It hits me with great force, as on other such occasions, that had I worked in such an environment, I would have been far happier. Were I to say this to my colleagues, many would say that I'm romanticizing the idea of being a small-town lawyer. They would mention the opportunities I would never have had if I had chosen such a workplace. And they would, of course, point out how much less money I would have earned if I had made such a decision. I will never know whether my colleagues' misgivings would have been right.

ᴥ ᴥ ᴥ

# Working in Different Places

I WOULD HAVE TO say that the diversity of Baltimore and the State of Maryland generally has been hospitable to my practice of law.

Maryland is sometimes referred to as "little America," because it contains nearly every type of topography found in this country. The state is bifurcated by the Chesapeake Bay and its tributaries, the largest contiguous estuary in the United States. For all intents and purposes Maryland's "Eastern Shore" is another state and has considered seceding from Maryland. The Eastern Shore borders the Atlantic Ocean and is best known for seafood, agricultural produce, and chickens.

The western part of Maryland includes a portion of the Appalachian mountain range. A large part of the state is farmland that suggests the Midwest. The only large city in Maryland is Baltimore, but the nation's capital, Washington, D.C., exists as if it were part of Maryland.

Maryland is divided by the Mason–Dixon line. Baltimore is in the northern part of the state, but barely so. During the Civil War, Baltimore and other parts of Maryland were divided between allegiances to the North and to the South. It was the state in which "brother fought brother."

Southern Maryland is largely a relic of the Old South and there are places where one might believe that the Civil War has just ended. Of all the parts of Maryland I have been to, I am least comfortable in Southern Maryland.

There are counties in Maryland where a city lawyer like me is encouraged to obtain "local counsel." On two occasions I failed to obey this warning and regretted it. One occasion took me to the northernmost county of Maryland, the other to the eastern edge of the Appalachian Mountains. In both instances, the local judge who entertained my case made it known to me that he did not welcome lawyers from the city. In one situation I survived the difficulty when, fortuitously, the judge learned that I was a friend of the managing partner of the law firm at which his son worked. In the other, I did badly in the case and have always felt I did my client a disservice by representing him without a local lawyer.

Usually when I have had work in another part of the state, I have driven there, sometimes for many hours. Such drives are useful for mental preparation on the way to the particular destination and enjoyable for scenery and mental wanderings on the way back.

One occasion I won't forget. I needed to visit a client in Cumberland, in the far western part of the state. I had to get there quickly, with an associate attorney of my law firm who was assisting me. The associate was reluctant to fly into the mountain town of Cumberland in the small airplane of Maryland's intrastate airline. I assured her that small airplanes were safer than cars, and our flights both ways were without incident. A few days later the plane we had been on crashed while making the same trip we had taken. All aboard were killed. I'm quite sure my estimation of the risks of flying in small planes was not taken seriously thereafter.

As I think back over many trips to places in Maryland where I have worked, certain types of experiences remain in my mind. I remember the day I went to a small community in Western Maryland to take a deposition. On arriving I was greeted by the clerk of the local court. He advised me that since the courtroom was not in use, we would be taking the deposition there. Recognizing that I was in unfamiliar surroundings, he then suggested that we have a cup of coffee while he explained the local customs.

I also remember the day I went to Southern Maryland, accompanied by my wife, to speak to a group of incoming students who were receiving scholarships to attend Cornell. The estate at which the event was held reminded me of Tara, the plantation in *Gone With The Wind*.

There was the time I had to interview witnesses in the Eastern Shore town of Cambridge to prepare for a trial. After interviewing the first witness at his place of business, I found that every other witness I visited knew who I was and what I was doing. A town network made known to everyone that a stranger had arrived, particularly if the stranger was from the big city.

When my work has taken me to a new place, particularly in a rural area, I always wonder what my life might have been had I lived in that place. I suppose I have such thoughts because, having grown up in a big city and worked and lived in several other big cities, the idea of living in a rural place seems mysterious and romantic. I have often wondered whether someone who grew up in such a place had similar feelings about living in a big city.

One difference between practicing law in a big city and in a small community came to me one day while I was selecting a jury in a court in northern Maryland. The judge made a remark I misheard as that he was surprised that he knew one of the prospective jurors. In fact, the judge had said that he was surprised that he didn't know one of the prospective jurors. I didn't understand that because the community in which the case was tried was so small the judge knew almost everyone called to serve. It never occurred to him that such familiarity might be inappropriate.

There is a county hospital client in a rural area that I drove to so often that I came to know houses, barns, and fields along the way. These landmarks became so familiar I eventually became wedded to particular thoughts as I came to each one. Each seemed to have captured its own synapses in my brain. Some of my thoughts concerned career choices I had made and whether they were wise or unwise. Some concerned particular clients and cases, evoking memories I enjoyed revisiting. Still others raised the perennial question of whether I had accomplished enough in my life.

When I had these thoughts I always wound up making a comparison that was not particularly flattering. I would compare my accomplishments to those of my stepfather. My stepfather was an extraordinary thoracic and cardiovascular surgeon of considerable renown, but this was not the basis of my comparison. The comparison concerns my stepfather's activities during World War II.

On June 6, 1944, my stepfather was in the landing in France (Normandy II, since he was a noncombatant). He was chief of surgery of a front-line evacuation hospital (the 102nd) for all five campaigns in the European theater (Normandy, Northern France, Ardennes, Rhineland, and Central Germany). He served when the city of Paris was reclaimed. He served during the Battle of the Bulge. He served at Remagen, when the bridge fell. He served at the liberation of Buchenwald. During his service, he ran the hospital, performed more than 700 open-body surgeries, supervised and sometimes conducted the triage, and, because his hospital was so far forward, dealt more than once with German soldiers and Gestapo officers. He was awarded a bronze star for staying with the wounded who could not be moved when his hospital fell behind enemy lines as the Germans advanced.

On anniversaries of the coldest days of the Battle of the Bulge my stepfather would sit on my parents' sun porch, shivering and remembering. I was privileged to hear his stories, many beyond imagination. When my stepfather died, I inherited photographs he took during the war, including those taken inside Buchenwald on the day it was liberated, log books, newspaper articles, and maps showing the directions of General Eisenhower.

I often thought about this on my way to engagements, and I felt puny. At such times, I thought about being showered and nicely dressed in my air-conditioned car, driving through gorgeous countryside to argue legal points, prepare documents, or talk with people about a case. Such activities cannot be measured against running a front-line evacuation hospital or performing major surgery on a battlefield or participating in the liberation of a concentration camp. I felt as though I was going to the movies and seeing the short but missing the main feature. During such musings I would tell myself that I was not responsible for being born too late to have had such experiences. Sometimes this relieved me slightly, but it never did the whole job.

❧ ❧ ❧

# Effect of Money

I JUST RECEIVED A telephone call of the sort that will bother me all day. The caller was referred by someone I know well. He and his wife are being sued for a considerable sum of money and, from what he told me, they have an arguable defense. Unfortunately, the defense would be very costly.

Although I would not have raised the matter of legal fees until the end of our first meeting, on the phone the caller himself brought it up. His question could not be deferred, since it was obvious that he wanted an answer before meeting me. I told him there's no way our law firm could handle the case other than on the customary hourly basis plus costs. I told him we would bill him for services monthly and, at his request, I offered a rough estimate of the total cost for the complete case. I assured him that I would use the leanest possible staff consistent with doing the job effectively. Finally, I told him the hourly rates of the partner, associate attorney, and paralegal who would work on his case. When I finished there was a long pause followed by a deep sigh. "I'll call you back," the caller said, and of course he did not.

The worst thing about practicing law is money. Money warps every decision lawyers make. Lawyers reject clients with worthy causes because they don't have enough money to pay legal fees. Lawyers accept clients they would rather not accept because they have plenty of money. For a sufficiently affluent client a lawyer can do everything conceivable to bring about a satisfactory result. For a client with limited funds a lawyer must cut corners. Often victory in a lawsuit or commercial matter goes to the party with the deepest pockets. There are times when clients settle for an unsatisfactory result because they cannot afford to continue paying legal fees. Every lawyer struggles with these pressures. If a lawyer tells you he hasn't made compromises on account of money, you've found a dishonest lawyer and should look for another.

ﺏ  ﺏ  ﺏ

# Free Will

THE CLIENT WHO IS about to arrive, a real estate developer, isn't a model citizen. He takes advantage of people. He takes things that don't belong to him. He lies. Sometimes I feel like telling him how offensive he is, but that isn't my job. I hold myself back.

There's something about many real estate developers that's distasteful to me. I don't like the way they look at things in their work. A person who looks at a beautiful farm and sees only its potential for lots for barren tract homes seems to me to be missing something important, an aesthetic sense of things.

I was watching the Charlie Rose Show last night and thinking about the meeting with my client about to take place. For the whole week, Charlie Rose has dedicated his show to neuroscience. His guests have been people who do research concerning different regions of the brain. The guests have been very knowledgeable. They included Nobel Prize winners and other scientists working at the cutting edge of neuroscience.

One of the themes of the Charlie Rose Shows this week has been the evolving association between different regions of the brain and different forms of behavior. It is reasonably well established that certain strong qualities such as sexual preference or the potential for violence are associated with discrete regions of the brain. Neuroscience has not yet reached the point where specific cells of the brain can be identified with different qualities, but the regions of the brain involved are becoming clear. It is only a question of time before neuroscientists are able to identify the specific groups of cells that are responsible for a person's conduct.

What if the day arrives when a lawyer tells the judge in a case against his client for breaching a contract, "Your Honor, my client's disregard of his responsibilities under the contract was due to a deficient ganglion in his amygdala. I will provide expert testimony that directly associates the deficient ganglion with his inability to meet obligations"? Or suppose a lawyer bargaining with another lawyer about a proposed provision in a legal document could say, "Susan, we will need to redefine paragraph 17(c)(ii) of the Indenture because my client tends to exaggerate his response to such contingencies. You see, Susan, Mr. Thompson's basal cortex is overdeveloped. Its anterior quadrant contains many times the normal number of cells." What is the judge or the other lawyer going to do in such situations?

The idea that specific conduct is controlled by forces out of a person's control is not new. B. F. Skinner wrote extensively about this in his 1971 book *Beyond Freedom and Dignity*. Skinner explained how decisions that appear to be the product of free will may, instead, be constrained by limitations over which people have no control. Skinner's idea may suggest that constraints upon free will have specific relationships to regions of the brain. For example, certain regions of the brain are associated with technical thinking and others with emotional reasoning. Now neuroscientists are able to explain how a person's reliance on one region or another affects that person's outlook and therefore conduct.

If my hypothetical situations appear a long way from the normal role of lawyers, it is interesting to note that the law has already recognized an important limitation on one's control in a particular situation. That situation is where a criminal defendant seeks to be excused from criminal conduct on the ground of insanity. Until the middle of the twentieth century, criminal insanity turned on whether a defendant was "able to appreciate the nature and quality of his actions." In other words, sanity depended upon cognitive ability.

As the psychology behind conduct matured, the test for sanity in many jurisdictions was changed to include a determination of whether the defendant's conduct "was the product of a mental disease or defect." In other words, the law changed to recognize that criminal insanity could be based upon either lack of cognition or lack of control. It is not a great leap for law to recognize other, less dramatic forms of conduct as attributable to involuntary brain function.

As my real estate developer client arrives, I must end my musing and get busy working on documents he needs for his business. In our discussion, nothing will be said about the possibility that aspects of my client's brain affect what he does.

I know I'm judgmental about my client. He would not appreciate the observation that his moral and aesthetic bankruptcy may be due to the way his brain evolved. Were I to mention this thought, he would doubtless glance at his clunky gold Rolex watch and tell me impatiently we don't have time for such speculation.

🐦 🐦 🐦

# Microcosm

THERE IS A WINDOW I see from the desk in my house where I work. Beyond it is a small patio and within it an unpaved square of land approximately four feet on each side. My wife planted bushes there years ago, and grasses have filled it in. I have been looking at this little garden for many years.

The ecology of the garden is extraordinary. After all the years of looking at it, I feel I am only now beginning to understand it. The butterflies that visit it have a distinct preference for one particular bush. The bees, however, prefer another. Caterpillars crawl up the vines entwined in some of the bushes and small birds land on the bushes from time to time. Occasionally frogs enter the garden for a short stay and on special occasions a praying mantis honors me with its presence. Only once have I seen the spider that makes cobwebs between two of the branches. Of course, I see only what occurs above ground.

I understand that each species in the garden occupies its own ecological niche. For each plant and animal to survive it must have the correct temperature, wind, moisture, salinity, and nourishment. There are elaborate relationships between the various plants and animals. Some provide the nourishment or habitat needed by others. Some require the assistance of other species to flourish. The complexity of what goes on in so small a space transfixes me.

I am sitting at my desk alone completing a finite task I have elected to do. Nothing of great importance depends upon my work. Outside my window, a few feet away, myriad living creatures are engaged in an intricate dance on which their existence depends. I wonder who decided to have this happen.

ða ða ða

# Architecture and Law

ACROSS THE STREET FROM my office is a stately mid-rise building, constructed in the early twentieth century as a railroad company's headquarters. The building reminds me of the work of Chicago architect Louis Sullivan. Despite its plebeian purpose, its architect refused to forego ornamentation. Touches of grace—modest fenestration around the windows, an ornate frieze and sensitive spacing and proportions—inform the building's design. The poignancy of the building's aesthetics is somehow emphasized by the banality of its purpose.

A particular feature of the building has captured my attention for a long time: the corner of the building at one of Baltimore's main intersections is not the customary right angle. Instead, the architect truncated the corner, thus enlarging the public space adjoining the intersection by setting the corner back at a forty-five degree angle. If Sullivan was correct that "form ever follows function," the architect must have envisioned the building's function as more than utilitarian.

I have often imagined a conversation between the architect and the sort of real estate developer frequently encountered today. The architect, whom I have named Samuel Weathersby, visits his developer client, Clyde Wormsley, to bring him plans for the building. The plans show the truncated corner Weathersby has designed and include stick figures engaged in conversation in front of the building.

Weathersby explains to Wormsley how the broad face of the building set back from the corner affords generosity to the street life around the building. He explains how a pointed corner discourages social interaction. He speaks passionately about the need for informal public gathering spaces and the responsibility of architects and developers to create them. He tells Wormsley that architecture is not simply a programmatic undertaking but has an aspirational component as well.

Wormsley's cell phone buzzes several times while Weathersby is speaking, but he hears him out without interruption. When Weathersby finishes speaking, Wormsley takes a deep breath and collects himself to respond. Wormsley's expression is a mixture of disbelief and revulsion. He can not believe someone he is paying is telling him such things.

"Sam," Wormsley begins, "have you gone crazy? Have you gone fucking crazy? Your plan throws away square footage on every floor and makes the best offices on the front corner totally ridiculous. Your job is to get every rentable square foot of office space out of this site. If you can get more space by pushing the FAR (floor area ratio) by setbacks, wedding-caking or anything else, do it. If you can get more space by cutting down the public factor with smaller elevators or tighter bathrooms, do it. In other words, Sam, your job is simple: squeeze the shit out of the numbers and give me a plan that I can make money on. If you want to do social work—talk about public spaces, aspirations and things like that— get a job as a social worker. If you want to be an architect, leave that stuff for someone else."

The point of the imaginary conversation between architect and developer is that there was no such conversation. The old railroad building was built before it became necessary to quantify everything. It was built before the exigencies and complexities of modern commerce overtook values not measurable in numbers. When the old railroad building was built, our society did not so easily eschew aesthetic and social considerations. The real Samuel Weathersby did not have to justify the truncated corner. My secret concordance with him reminds me—sometimes even as I glance at the corner in the midst of work with a client—that we were once richer in ways that never can be measured.

ク ク ク

# Is It Right?

WHEN I ATTENDED FIELDSTON High School, we had a class each year known simply as "Ethics." Once a week we would go up narrow stairs to a small room and seat ourselves in a semicircle around the teacher. The class had no homework, no grades, and no effect on our consuming concern to get into a good college.

At the beginning of each Ethics class, the teacher suggested a topic: "Why don't we discuss euthanasia?" or "Let's discuss lying today." After brief introductory remarks, the teacher would turn to the students and ask the question of the day. The question was asked in different forms, but always came down to "Is it right?"

Each student was given the opportunity to respond to the question. Some students spoke briefly, saying merely yes, maybe, or no; some had nothing to say. Others spoke at length, explaining the circumstances under which something might be right or wrong, the relevance of intentions, the possibility of different understandings.

After our answers, we left the small room and walked down the narrow stairs to our other classes. There was no summation, no attempt to reach consensus, no closure of any kind. I came away from Ethics class with no answers.

Since high school life has gone well for me: college and law school, a judicial clerkship, four years as a federal prosecutor, and thirty years in a practice that has grown and prospered. My family life has gone well and we have two terrific children. To my colleagues, clients, family, and friends, it appears I have answered the important questions.

Recently I was handling a thorny contract matter for a client. My adversary was not experienced in such matters and he made a serious mistake that prejudiced his client. I did what a lawyer is expected to do in such circumstances. I took full advantage of my colleague's inexperience.

Not long after the matter was concluded, I began questioning what I had done. Should a lawyer do whatever is necessary to win a dispute, even if it means taking advantage of a less experienced lawyer? Would I have been unfair to my client if I had telephoned my adversary and suggested off the record that he might want to reconsider his position? As has happened many times, after a matter has ended and the who-struck-johns are over, I am left with a nagging question, "Is it right?"

I wonder if among the questions I have answered I have overlooked some important ones. I have often wanted to ask a client mindlessly pursuing money or power "Is it right?" I have often wanted to ask a friend or colleague making an expedient decision "Is it right?" And I have often asked myself about choices I have made—to act or not act, to speak or not speak, to care or not care—"Is it right?" I think after all this time I'm still coming down narrow stairs from a small room, from Ethics class, with no answers.

ða  ða  ða

# You Don't Need a Lawyer

I WROTE A BOOK titled *You Don't Need A Lawyer*. There are a lot of people who would prefer never to see a lawyer, so the book has been reasonably popular. Unfortunately, the title of the book has two limitations.

The first limitation is that the title does not mean you'll never need a lawyer for anything. There are many things that can be handled without a lawyer if done properly. I won't explain those matters here, but if you're interested, see the book.

The other limitation doesn't concern the range of matters that can be handled without a lawyer. It concerns the diligence required to obtain a good result. The work must be done diligently. Sometimes, people are not willing to do this.

From time to time, I have occasion to discuss both these limitations with people who call me. The first one is fairly easy to address. I simply explain that the book is useful for many everyday situations, but does not do away with the need for a lawyer in other situations, in particular, a case that is serious or large. Most people understand this limitation and can determine from the types of cases discussed the scope of the book.

The second limitation is more difficult to explain. The book deals with forms of letters that are likely to bring about a desired result, and a person who uses the book's advice needs to be prepared to write such letters. Some of the suggestions I make are easy to follow, such as to send letters by certified mail, with return receipt requested. Other suggestions, such as using statements of experts or competitors, require some thought. I find it frustrating that people who do not follow the suggestions carefully could obtain the results they want if they did so. I wish I could write a book that would make success possible with no effort, but I can't do so.

This is the sort of phone call I occasionally receive:

"I got your book about doing things without a lawyer. The problem I'm having is that I bought a lawnmower that doesn't work and the store won't take it back."

"Have you read the part of the book that deals with defective merchandise?"

"I read some of it, but I don't have all day to read law books."

"The book is not a law book and the part dealing with defective merchandise is fairly short. Why don't you read it and see if you can write a letter as the book suggests?"

"If I tell you what went on, could you write the letter for me?"

"No, I don't write letters for people who aren't my clients, and I don't want clients who have your sort of problem. I wrote the book so that people like you could solve problems without a lawyer."

I can't help a caller like this one. What he wants is free legal assistance and he may well have wasted his money buying my book. The best I can do for people like him is to encourage them to follow the suggestions in the book. There's no such thing as a how-to book that doesn't require readers to make a serious effort to follow what it suggests.

Ȥ Ȥ Ȥ

# Thoughts About *Nighthawks*

I'M WORKING TONIGHT ON a complicated matter. My client and his fellow stockholders are selling a business that manufactures a sophisticated product. The stockholders, who do not entirely agree on everything, reside in several different countries. The product is manufactured in China and sold throughout most of the world. There are contracts with suppliers, customers, banks, and businesses that cooperate with my client's business. The nature of the sale of the business involves many aspects of each contract. I have made a diagram of the contracts and indicated on it how they will change when the sale is accomplished.

The sale will require seven or eight complicated documents that are still in draft form and a handful of relatively minor documents. The drafts of the complicated documents have made the rounds of lawyers, who have added their comments and proposed changes to them. My job tonight is to determine which of my colleagues' proposed changes are acceptable, which are not acceptable, and which can be made acceptable with certain revisions. On a scale of one to ten for the complexity of jobs I do, tonight's work would score at least nine.

On the wall of my office is a reproduction of Edward Hopper's *Nighthawks*. It has been in my office for years and I have studied it assiduously. People who know painting far better than I do often comment that the two geniuses of light are Vermeer and Hopper. I can't vouch for Vermeer but if *Nighthawks* were Hopper's only painting I could vouch for him. Hopper's use of light in *Nighthawks* is nothing short of incredible. Every detail of the painting, the counters and bar stools, the faces and clothing of the counterman and customers, the floors, the walls, the napkin holders, and countless other items and even the dark shops barely visible across the street are suffused with light at precisely correct angles and intensities.

There have been times when I have gone up to the painting and studied a few square inches of it. Each time I see the labor, perhaps the anguish, that Hopper put into his work. Surely he said to himself that *Nighthawks* would be perfect or as perfect as he could make it. From where I am sitting surrounded by documents and yellow legal pads I can see some of these details.

If I do everything that could be done with the legal documents in this transaction, if I could do them as perfectly as Hopper painted *Nighthawks*, there would be two ineradicable differences between our work. The first, of course, is that *Nighthawks* is a glorious, epiphanic creation, and a stack of legal documents would never deserve that description. Second, the product of Hopper's precision plainly demonstrates to any sentient person the effort that went into it.

To most people, including most clients, my final product will be only the accomplishment of a particular transaction. At best a few of my colleagues may comprehend the work that went into it. If the transaction is successful, my client won't care if it was accomplished by the best set of documents any lawyer ever prepared or scribbles on toilet paper. Hopper's product is intended to fill needs for aesthetic gratification. Mine is intended to fill bank accounts.

But in another respect it is Hopper, not I, who gets a pass on revealing himself.

Someone apparently wrote an article in which Edward Hopper was described as having an unpleasant personality. I didn't read that article but I read another article that commented upon it. The author of the article I read contended that Hopper was a delightful person and that the Hoppers had long been personal friends with him and his wife. I understand why a friend of Hopper might want to set the record straight, but my response to the friend's article was that Hopper's personality makes no difference. Hopper's *Nighthawks*, or any other painting, says all that needs to be said about the artist. The artist could live in ignominy for all his personality matters.

My situation is entirely different. My personality is relevant to the success of my work with clients, colleagues, and others. I must interact successfully to obtain the information and understanding necessary to be sure I am on the right track in a particular matter. I must explain to my clients what I do and inform them about how my work is intended to bring about a successful conclusion. Without these interactions a perfect set of documents could never accomplish its purpose.

One other thing comes to mind as I look up from my tedious work and delight once again in *Nighthawks*. Although our reasons may differ, Hopper could not skip steps in his work, and neither can I. In my case, and I suspect in Hopper's, this is not simply out of a desire to succeed in particular undertakings. There is something in my mind, as I suspect there was in Hopper's, that makes me feel as though I'm being watched and judged by an omnipotent power. If I'm correct, the great artist and I have something in common.

ᓫ ᓫ ᓫ

# Teaching Law

YEARS AGO I TAUGHT two courses at two different law schools. The results of these experiences were surprising and instructive.

One course was environmental law. I had agreed to fill in for a colleague on sabbatical. I was familiar with the subject because I had tried a number of cases involving water pollution in marshlands. I could have taught the course in the traditional way, basing it on legislation and court decisions, but I chose to do otherwise. What I tried to accomplish in the course was to explain how the law expands and contracts to accommodate or discourage emerging technologies.

The centerpiece of this effort was a book* I had studied in law school on decisions of the Supreme Judicial Court of Massachusetts in the mid-nineteenth century, during the tenure of Chief Justice Shaw. At that time major technological changes, particularly the railroad, were emerging. In a series of decisions written by the Chief Justice the law pertaining to such diverse matters as eminent domain, taxation, and torts was rendered more hospitable to encouraging these developments than it might have been without such shadings.

From the outset, the students in the class were unimpressed with this approach. Some asked me repeatedly, "What is the law in that situation?," to which I responded repeatedly that the specific law in particular situations was not of importance in this discussion. The students' discomfort increased during the semester and my evaluations at its conclusion were abysmal. In the opinion of one student I shouldn't be teaching in law school.

The other course was taught entirely differently. With a dean's generous permission, I designed it in a way I had always wanted to try, using the business school model of beginning discussions with a concrete empirical situation, then introducing the legal principles that applied to it. As I recall, the first situation explored was that of a married couple who owned a small housewares store situated on the main street of a mid-size town. When the nature of shopping in the community changed the couple had to move their store to a shopping center. As a result, they had to address the complexities of a lease in a shopping center, new insurance

---

*Levy, *The Law of the Commonwealth and Chief Justice Shaw* (1957).

requirements, various regulatory constraints, and new considerations regarding their two employees, along with other matters.

I had hoped to cover five situations in the course, but was barely able to cover three. The students were clearly interested in what was discussed, and classes were lively and satisfying. At the end of the semester my evaluations were excellent. For one student the course was the best taken in law school.

Certain aspects of the two courses may have contributed to the students' receptions. The first course was a professor-stands-in-front-of-the-class-at-a-lectern, no-drinking-or-eating course; the second was taught on Saturday mornings around a table, in seminar fashion, with food and drinks permitted. But I doubt that these aspects accounted for the vast difference in the students' responses. Since my teaching ability (or inability) was essentially the same in both courses, it could not have explained what occurred.

I believe the difference was largely attributable to my failure in the first course to provide a comprehensible setting for the legal principles that were discussed. Legal principles are devoid of meaning until they are applied to real situations of real people in the real world. What we call "law" is what results from the application of principles to facts. In the second course the students appreciated the facts of a situation presented to them before legal principles were introduced. When applied to those facts the principles became meaningful in human affairs. It is not an exaggeration to say that everyone who thinks about law wants to know how it affects people as they conduct their affairs.

ια ια ια

# The Best Lawyers

ONE OF MY PARTNERS walks into my office, squinting like a prisoner just released from the black hole. Slowly, he looks around the room, fixing his gaze on various objects as though he had never seen them before. Since he has been in my office dozens of times, I'm confused by his demeanor.

Having completed his survey, with his eyes almost closed my partner asks his question: "Who are the best lawyers you've ever known?"

I give this some thought and then ask: "Can I change the question?"

"What's the change?"

"I'd rather tell you what I think are the most important qualities of a good lawyer."

"OK," my partner responds, "and then I'm going to ask you which lawyers have those qualities."

We've arrived at a conundrum: The best lawyers are those who have the most important qualities and those qualities determine which lawyers are the best.

"I give up," I say to my partner, "I'll give you two names: Arthur Liman and Brendan Sullivan."

Now my partner comes to my question: "What qualities make them the best lawyers?"

"It's not any one particular skill or even a combination of skills. I know lawyers who can draft as well as Arthur or Brendan. I know lawyers who can organize materials as well as they can. I know lawyers who can argue to courts and juries as well as either of them. But Arthur and Brendan have three qualities that very few other lawyers possess."

"What are they?"

"The first is that these guys absolutely believe in their cases from the moment they accept a client. From the first moment they simply don't acknowledge the possibility they won't succeed. This overriding conviction becomes a self-fulfilling prophesy as the case proceeds."

"What's the second quality?"

"There's absolutely nothing in a client's interest that's too small to deserve consummate attention. If a witness is of almost no significance, the witness gets interviewed numerous times and shaped-up as though he or she will provide pivotal evidence in the case. If there's a possibility that a scrap of evidence could be found under a rock in Bangladesh, an associate is sent to Bangladesh with instructions to turn the rock over and look for the evidence. Anyone who can't take that sort of thing, better not work for one of these guys."

"What's the third quality?"

"The third quality is thinking outside the box. Lawyers like Brendan and Arthur not only consider every known possibility for winning their cases, they also conceive of solutions no one has ever thought of before. I've worked with Brendan more than once when a solution he conceived was so novel it was almost laughable, laughable, that is, until it worked."

My partner finally opens his eyes fully and looks me in the face: "So those are the three characteristics of a great lawyer."

"You've got it. Let's get back to work." ★

---

★Consideration of the "best" lawyers raises a matter apart from the quality of a lawyer's practice. This matter is that those lawyers who are considered for such distinction are invariably at the top of the socioeconomic spectrum. Although there are lawyers in small towns and neighborhood offices who are excellent practitioners (and lawyers in prominent law firms who have no idea how to practice), such lawyers are not included in discussions about the "best" lawyers. The field on which such judgments are made is not level.

ᕮᕮ ᕮᕮ ᕮᕮ

# Jurors From Different Worlds

THIS SMALL INCIDENT STAYS in my memory.

I had just completed a trial that I used to train a young lawyer. I don't remember what the case was about, who the judge was, or even which young lawyer I was training. I don't even remember the verdict, although I have a vague feeling we won.

What I do remember, as a moment frozen in time, is something that took place after the trial ended. I had asked jurors who were agreeable to remain in their seats after the judge discharged them, so that they could help me with training. I had given the young lawyer the opportunity to examine a witness, to cross-examine another witness, and to respond to some objections. I'm sure the jury figured out what was happening.

I recall many of the jurors remained in their seats, as requested. For the young lawyer's benefit I questioned them about his performance at the trial. On the extreme right-hand side of the jury box was a white man carefully groomed and wearing an expensive suit, shirt and necktie and a pair of Italian loafers. I even recall the tasteful rectangular wristwatch he wore. According to the jury information sheet he was a 56-year-old businessman who lived in an affluent suburb of Washington, D.C.

On the extreme left-hand side of the jury box sat a black man wearing well-worn overalls. The jury information sheet identified him as a 48-year-old farmer who lived in a small rural community in southern Maryland. His hands, visible on the back of the chair in front of him, told everything one needed to know about his work. I was familiar with the small community where he lived. It had remained segregated long after the law prohibited that. A majority of the black people in that community were descendants of slaves who made their living as the functional equivalent of sharecroppers.

These two jurors couldn't have been more different. They were white and black, wealthy and poor, well-educated and probably not so, one a resident of a wealthy metropolitan community and the other of a poor rural community. One of the men was dressed impeccably, the other wore soiled work clothes. These men would never have encountered one another but for the fortuity of serving on the same jury. These men would never have had equal power but for the fact that each had only one vote for the verdict.

The incident that is fixed in my mind consumed perhaps a half-minute. The white man, replying to a question I had asked, looked across the jury box directly into the face of the black man and, for an instant, they were simply two men sharing an experience. For that instant they were shorn of all incidents of social status. They were equals for that instant. The white man said, "One of the things that persuaded me to vote as I did was the point Mr. Washington made about timing. He showed us it wasn't possible for the events to have occurred any other way."

# CHAPTER FOUR

# Lessons

LAW CONCERNS THE APPLICATION of principles to facts. Therefore, lawyers have to acquire full knowledge of all the facts relevant to a client's case. This is not always a simple matter. Some facts can be acquired by interviewing clients or examining physical evidence. My early morning visit to the freezer with the owner of my meatpacking client provided the knowledge that made a successful conclusion of the case possible.

Other facts, particularly those about how a person behaves in different situations, frequently are not available to lawyers through deliberate means. These facts are often gleaned from clients' stories, from serendipitous incidents, neither planned nor expected. Because clients are usually available and, one hopes, cooperative, it is advisable, within the limitations of time and expense, to interview them extensively. The attorney–client privilege, if properly understood by a client, should allay fears that candor about incriminating or embarrassing matters may be harmful to the client.

As this collection of essays indicates, the special nature of a lawyer's relationship to a client allows clients to willingly reveal that they have been dishonest or performed defective work or been emotionally overwhelmed by a case or too embarrassed, sad or anxious to testify meaningfully. A client may even be able to reveal having contemplated suicide or engaging in sexual misconduct or having two de facto marriages. Although it may require several interviews, such information is usually available from a client.

The essays in this book suggest that I am inclined to view circumstances and feelings through a rather wide lens. Although usually this has benefitted me in my practice, it has not always done so, as the following two situations make clear.

In the first situation, I was retained by a husband and wife to review construction and architectural contracts for a new house on the bank of a river near Annapolis, the capital of Maryland. Many things about the project interested me, and I expressed my thoughts about the ecology of the area, architectural possibilities, and the history of Annapolis. My comments were almost always met by silence and I failed, to my later regret, to understand that my clients were not interested in such digressions. After a few weeks, the wife advised me that she and her husband would call if they wanted anything further. They never did, and I learned from a colleague that the couple wanted to discuss nothing but essential legal information.

In the second situation, I visited a client on a resort island where he was living with his family for the purpose of acquiring specific information pertinent to his case. During the first two days, at several meals and other times, I tried unsuccessfully to question my client about the relevant matter. On the third and final day of my visit, we began talking about life on the island. We discussed its politics, transportation, amenities, and the availability of medical care. At one point I compared an aspect of life on the island to something I had come to visit my client to learn. My client delved into this comparison and, from that moment on, he freely discussed the facts I needed to acquire. These and many other experiences have taught me to approach digressions cautiously to determine whether a client is receptive to them.

Lawyers also need to acquire facts from people other than clients. In most circumstances such people are not compelled to speak with lawyers. Frequently, however, random encounters with such people yield relevant information. These incidents may be of determinative value in a particular case.

I doubt whether the result that occurred in my defense of the young woman check forger would have been possible without the encounters with officials involved in her case. I am certain that without the relationship I developed with the arresting officer the judge's crucial acceptance of an unusual request on behalf of my young client would not have been possible.

Such incidents are particularly valuable when a person with useful knowledge in a case is loath to speak with a lawyer. Not infrequently, knowing that information will be used in a legal matter makes a person reluctant to reveal it. In such instances, people's stories may provide valuable information that might otherwise not be obtained.

There are situations in which a planned encounter provides little or no useful information, but a resulting incidental encounter may prove to be productive. More than once, when I visited banks with prosecutors I was training to interview tellers present during an armed robbery, the tellers provided no useful information. A clerk or janitor, however, advised us of the location of fingerprints or a hidden camera that took photographs of the robbers. Particularly when a large number of people may have relevant information, a visit to the site of an event may provide an unlikely source of information about a case.

In some situations knowledge acquired in talking to people can prevent lawyers from encountering a fatal pitfall. This happened to an adversary of mine. The defendant in a tax fraud case I prosecuted was alleged to have failed to report substantial income. The defendant contended that such information was provided to his accountant who had failed to incorporate it in his tax return. The crucial exhibit was a group of worksheets the defendant contended he had provided to the accountant. The defendant testified that page 7 showed the allegedly omitted income. That page was typed using the same kind of paper and the same typewriter as all the other pages.

The crucial question my unprepared adversary asked the accountant was, "Mr. Kemper, how can you possibly contend that page number 7 in this exhibit was not in the papers you received?" Mr. Kemper, a shy and careful witness, gave the answer which won the case: "When I was in college I worked for the American Standard Paper Company in Oregon. I learned from my job that watermarks on paper are shot through the particular stack on a diagonal. As a result, the watermark on each page is slightly to the side of the watermark on the preceding page."

The witness then put the worksheets in front of a lightbox so that the jury could see the watermarks on each page. All of the watermarks fell on a perfect diagonal, except for page 7. The page 7 the defendant had produced at trial was clearly not the page 7 he had provided to his accountant. Had my adversary gone further afield in studying the background of Mr. Kemper, who he knew would be an important witness, he would not have walked into the disaster that befell him.

Experience shows lawyers that it is important to make judgments about others slowly. It is tempting to assume, for example, that people of great prominence and wealth are not sensitive to those who do not enjoy such fortune. In my work I have seen striking examples of situations in which this assumption was proven false. I have seen the chief executive officer of a national financial institution, at a social gathering in a private home, go out of his way to relieve the embarrassment of a domestic worker.

I was invited to the apartment of an NFL quarterback in mid-season to prepare for his deposition in a case in which he was a fortuitous witness to a situation involving a client with very little financial means. The quarterback undertook with alacrity the assistance of my client in a matter involving financial consequences of less than one percent of his salary. Unplanned and unexpected incidents have taught me to withhold uncharitable prejudices until more is known about an individual.

Incidents in the nature of backstories can be surprising in disappointing ways. A client I believed to be gregarious and nonjudgmental came to me and asked for my assistance in terminating a contract he had entered into to purchase a new house. After pleasantries and a brief discussion about my client's future plans, he asked me a shocking question: could he cancel the contract because the seller of the house defrauded him by not advising him that a neighboring house was occupied by a family of a religious persuasion not acceptable to him?

There was an occasion when, while I was visiting a building of concern to a small group of wealthy businessmen, a custodian walked up to me and asked for my help. The custodian told me, and I later confirmed, that my clients had engaged his overtime services for a minor matter but, despite his numerous requests, had failed to pay the small sum they had agreed to pay him. Incidents such as these are not only unplanned and unexpected, they are unwelcome as well.

Through such incidents one learns that surprises concerning people may be disappointing as well as gratifying. But, gratifying or not, they help a lawyer develop skills for dealing with idiosyncratic people. These incidents are of great value to lawyers, whose job it is to assist all sorts of clients to realize their objectives within the bounds of law, practicality, and ethics.

Lawyers also learn a great deal about their colleagues through behind-the-scenes encounters. Sometimes such information occurs in a particular case and, thereafter, lawyers who learn of what occurred will be prepared to deal with the other lawyer. Sometimes the information is simply general, but it is useful to lawyers in dealing with colleagues. Every lawyer wants to know whether an adversary is careful or not so, skilled or unskilled, honest or dishonest. Such things are rarely learned from a single experience with a lawyer, and such encounters provide a breadth of knowledge that enables one to make such determinations.

In addition to knowledge about clients, others, and lawyers, backstories make the work of lawyers far more interesting than it would be without them. They reveal the diversity and idiosyncracies of people. They broaden a lawyer's general knowledge.

I did not use in particular cases the backstory information I acquired by meeting a man who could design a planetarium; a man who island-hopped across the Pacific in one of the first airplanes ever seen in South-east Asia; or a seaman whose boat was struck by a giant rogue wave in mid-ocean. Nevertheless, such information added to my general under-standing and, I believe, made me a better lawyer.

I know my understanding of human affairs has been enriched by my knowledge that my former office mate played a heroic part in the civil rights movement and my knowledge of what transpired when the Vice President of the United States faced criminal charges in federal court. The information I acquired from such incidents had no bearing upon any cases I was handling, but greatly enhanced my ability to establish pro-ductive relationships with clients and others.

A common denominator of lawyers' reflections is that lawyers tend to contemplate a wide range of topics. This is probably due to the fact that lawyers do not limit their work to one field of interest because their clients in the aggregate pursue many fields. My own special interests—music, architecture, technology, books, truth and justice—arise regularly in activities of my clients and other aspects of my work. This is surely true for other practicing lawyers. In addition, since a purpose of law is to pro-vide a structure in which social activities may take place, it is difficult for a lawyer not to reflect upon how legal thinking and analysis bear upon arts and sciences, public policy, and philosophical concepts. Each of the reflections described in this book bears a relationship to people and ideas I have encountered in my work.

Years ago I served as chairman of a special committee of the Mary-land State Bar Association known as the Law Practice Quality Commit-tee. The organizer of this committee, a well-respected partner in one of Baltimore's oldest and largest law firms, created it for the purpose of exploring the extent to which clients were satisfied with the services of lawyers. Shortly after his untimely death, I became chairman. During my tenure, we explored the extent to which lawyers were satisfied with the profession they had chosen.

In order to acquire an independent measure of lawyers' satisfaction we procured the services of a firm with expertise in surveying preferences and attitudes. This consultant conducted interviews of many lawyers engaged in a variety of practices. The results were disquieting. They showed that a significant number of lawyers were dissatisfied with the practice of law and, in more than a few instances, wished they had not chosen law as a profession. When other state bar associations conducted similar studies the results were much the same.

I have often thought about the results of these surveys and why they were so disappointing. I doubt if the nature of the work or its financial compensation explain such results. What I think may be missing, in the practices of some of my colleagues, is openness to interesting and diverse incidents and people. My experience has been that the more expansive a lawyer's style of practice becomes, the more productive and gratifying it will be. It is difficult to be dissatisfied with one's work when one experiences unplanned and unexpected incidents of intrinsic interest. I am hopeful that the essays this book demonstrate that the practice of law affords such opportunities to lawyers who welcome them.

# Epilogue

THE ESSAYS COLLECTED HERE have certain elements in common.

The incidents from which the essays arose were unplanned. I did not expect a woman who came to my office to prepare a codicil to her will to bring with her, as it were, her deceased husband. I did not expect a straight-laced businessman to be overwhelmed by the thought of selling the family farm. I did not expect the captain of a Romanian fishing vessel to put before me a picture of his family to tell me what he was unable to say in English. Lawyers generally do not place much stock in serendipity, but behind-the-scenes events arise serendipitously. They are unplanned and unexpected. If the events in these essays had been expected, they would almost surely have affected me far less.

These events could have happened to anyone. They did not arise because of specialness of the people involved. The harsh and lonely life of a tugboat operator is understandable by anyone who can imagine his circumstances. The self-imposed rule of a Holocaust survivor against informing on others might be observed by anyone who suffered such an experience. No particular background or occupation makes a person interesting or admirable or boring or offensive. There are no particular characteristics of people who are given to playing "gotcha" with a lawyer. These qualities appear in people with every kind of history and background.

It was not my intent in this book to explain or criticize legal principles, even though occasionally I have slouched in that direction. Nor was it my intent to afford readers an understanding of the full facts of the cases in which the events arose. Most cases involve many facts, disputed and not disputed. Since law arises at the intersection of principles and facts, legal analysis of the cases would require far greater factual under-standing than reflected in these essays. I have endeavored to provide read-ers with sufficient facts to enable them to appreciate the context of the events described, and nothing more.

Since the work of lawyers has for the most part an inherent solem-nity, the events described stand in contrast to its general flow. When an event occurs that arouses passion, it is as though bright colors have been placed on a blank canvas. This book is about those colors against the can-vas of my experience as a lawyer.

## Acknowledgments

I COULD NOT HAVE written this book without the help of my assistant, Hilary Matzinger. Hilary not only prepared and organized the manuscript but her many suggestions about language and substance were invaluable. My editor (and sister) Ellin Sarot edited the entire manuscript. I was the beneficiary of Ellin's many years as an editor for Harvard University and *The New England Journal of Medicine*. My friends and distinguished colleagues, George Beall, Benjamin R. Civiletti, Stephen H. Sachs and Brendan V. Sullivan, have honored me by their generosity in reading and commenting upon the manuscript. Lawyers such as these assure it will always be a source of pride to be in the legal profession. Thanks to the ECF Reporter (Is it Right?), the Maryland State Bar Association (Where Have All the Books Gone?), and the Southampton Press (An Illegal Immigrant) for permitting use in this book of articles first published there. Thanks also to my friend Karen Capelluto, a talented and accomplished painter, for sharing with me her concept "noticings." Karen has enabled me to understand that emanations of small incidents are often more powerful than large events.

# About the Author

JAMES M. KRAMON IS a lawyer in the law firm of Kramon & Graham, P.A., Baltimore, Maryland, of which he is co-founder. He formerly served as a law clerk in the Tax Division of the Justice Department and for a United States Circuit Judge in Chicago. Thereafter, he served as an Assistant United States Attorney for four years. Mr. Kramon has taught at several law schools and published over seventy articles and six books. He holds degrees from Carnegie-Mellon University (B.S.), George Washington University (J.D. with Honors), Johns Hopkins University (M.L.A.), and Harvard Law School (LL.M).